The Art of Rela:
Stress Reduction and ~~~
Techniques

By

Harmony Grace

Vij Books
New Delhi (India)

Published by

Vij Books
(Publishers, Distributors & Importers)
4836/24, 3rd Floor, Ansari Road
Delhi – 110 002
Phone: 91-11-43596460
Mobile: 98110 94883
e-mail: contact@vijpublishing.com
www.vijbooks.in

ISBN: 978-81-19438-03-7 (PB)

The Art of Relaxation: Stress Reduction and Self-Care Techniques

Contents

Introduction to The Art of Relaxation

Navigating the Path to Inner Harmony

In the fast-paced rhythm of modern life, where stress has become an unwelcome companion, the pursuit of tranquility and well-being has never been more crucial. Welcome to "The Art of Relaxation," a guide crafted by Harmony Grace, a mindful expert dedicated to unraveling the secrets of stress reduction and self-care.

In the Symphony of Life, Seek Harmony:

Life, much like a symphony, is composed of various elements that contribute to its melody. Yet, amidst the demands of work, family, and personal aspirations, the harmony can often be drowned out by the dissonance of stress. This book serves as a guide to rediscovering that harmony, a roadmap to navigate the intricacies of relaxation and self-care.

Understanding the Essence of Relaxation:

In these pages, we embark on a journey to understand the very essence of relaxation. What does it mean to truly unwind in a world that seldom pauses? Harmony Grace invites you to redefine relaxation not merely as a luxury but as an art—a skill to be cultivated and integrated into the fabric of daily life.

The Impact of Stress on Well-Being:

Before we delve into the artistry of relaxation, it's essential to recognize the impact of stress on our well-being. The opening chapters shed light on the science behind stress, exploring its physical and psychological dimensions. Harmony Grace gently guides readers to identify personal stressors, laying the groundwork for a personalized approach to stress reduction.

Embarking on a Mind-Body Journey:

At the heart of this exploration lies the mind-body connection—a powerful force that, when nurtured, forms the cornerstone of relaxation. The introductory chapters unravel the intricacies of this relationship and introduce practices that harmonize the mind and body, setting the stage for a holistic approach to well-being.

Breathing Life into Relaxation:

Breath, often overlooked in the hustle of daily life, emerges as a powerful ally in the quest for relaxation. Harmony Grace introduces readers to the art of mindful breathing, laying the foundation for practices that transform each breath into a gateway to serenity.

The Canvas of Mindfulness:

Mindfulness, a key brushstroke in the art of relaxation, is explored as a transformative practice. Harmony Grace gently invites readers to embrace mindfulness meditation, guiding them through the process of building a practice that extends beyond the pages of this book.

Visualizing a Tapestry of Tranquility:

As the journey unfolds, the chapters on visualization and imagery invite readers to paint their mental retreats. Harmony Grace provides tools for crafting vivid mental landscapes that transport individuals to a realm of tranquility, regardless of external circumstances.

In the chapters that follow, readers will explore the power of progressive muscle relaxation, the healing embrace of yoga, the role of nutrition in relaxation, and a spectrum of self-care rituals. "The Art of Relaxation" is not just a guide; it is an invitation to embark on a transformative journey—an exploration of the profound impact that the art of relaxation can have on our lives. So, let us begin this odyssey towards inner harmony, where the canvas of serenity awaits your unique strokes.

Defining Relaxation and its Importance:
A Prelude to Inner Harmony

In the tapestry of life, relaxation is the thread that weaves moments of calm and tranquility into the chaotic rhythm of our daily existence. As we embark on the journey of "The Art of Relaxation," understanding the essence of relaxation becomes the foundation upon which we build a sanctuary of well-being. Let us delve into the very definition of relaxation and explore why it is a fundamental key to inner harmony.

Defining Relaxation:

At its core, relaxation is not merely a state of physical ease; it is a profound and intentional release of tension on multiple levels—physical, mental, and emotional. It is a conscious choice to step back from the hurried pace of life, inviting a sense of calm that permeates the body, mind, and spirit. Relaxation is not a passive state; rather, it is an artful practice that requires mindfulness and a deliberate shift in focus.

In the context of "The Art of Relaxation," defining relaxation extends beyond the absence of activity. It embraces a dynamic stillness—a state where the mind unwinds, muscles soften, and the spirit finds solace. It is a deliberate act of self-care, a pause in the relentless pursuit of productivity, and a return to the present moment.

The Importance of Relaxation:

Understanding the importance of relaxation is akin to recognizing the vital role it plays in nurturing holistic well-being. In a world characterized by constant stimuli and perpetual motion, the significance of intentional relaxation cannot be overstated.

Stress Reduction: Relaxation serves as a powerful antidote to stress. When stressors abound, the body's stress response is triggered, leading to physiological and psychological tension. Through intentional relaxation, this tension is released, allowing the body and mind to return to a state of equilibrium.

Physical Health: The impact of relaxation on physical health is profound. Chronic stress has been linked to a myriad of health issues, from cardiovascular problems to weakened immune function. By prioritizing relaxation, individuals fortify their bodies against the detrimental effects of prolonged stress.

Mental Clarity and Focus: A relaxed mind is more conducive to clarity and focus. When tension dissipates, cognitive function improves, fostering enhanced problem-solving abilities, creativity, and the capacity to navigate challenges with a clear perspective.

Emotional Well-Being: Emotionally, relaxation acts as a balm for the spirit. It cultivates emotional resilience, reduces anxiety, and provides a sanctuary for processing and understanding emotions. This emotional well-being, in turn, strengthens interpersonal relationships and one's overall outlook on life.

Quality of Sleep: Relaxation plays a pivotal role in fostering restful and rejuvenating sleep. By unwinding before bedtime, individuals create a conducive environment for the body and mind to enter a state of deep relaxation, promoting quality sleep.

Lifestyle Balance: Intentional relaxation is the cornerstone of a balanced lifestyle. It encourages individuals to carve out moments for self-care, promoting a sustainable and fulfilling way of living.

As we embark on this exploration of relaxation, let us bear in mind its definition not as a passive state, but as an intentional and dynamic practice—a cornerstone of well-being that holds the key to unlocking inner harmony in our journey through life.

The Impact of Stress on Well-Being: Navigating the Tumultuous Terrain

In the intricate dance of life, stress often emerges as an uninvited partner, disrupting the harmony of our physical, mental, and emotional well-being. As we embark on the journey of "The Art of Relaxation," it is imperative to understand the profound impact that stress can wield on our overall well-being.

The Physiology of Stress:

Stress, in its evolutionary origins, served as a survival mechanism, triggering the body's "fight or flight" response to imminent threats. In contemporary society, however, the stressors have evolved from immediate physical dangers to complex, ongoing challenges. The body's response, however, remains deeply ingrained—an intricate interplay of hormonal and physiological changes designed to prepare us for swift action.

When stress is chronic and pervasive, as is often the case in modern life, the constant activation of the stress response takes a toll on the body. The release of stress hormones such as cortisol and adrenaline, intended for short-term emergencies, becomes a chronic cascade that disrupts the delicate balance of bodily functions.

Physical Ramifications of Chronic Stress:

Cardiovascular System: Chronic stress is a known contributor to cardiovascular issues. The continuous release of stress hormones can elevate blood pressure, increase heart rate, and contribute to the buildup of arterial plaque. Over time, this can lead to conditions such as hypertension and an increased risk of heart disease.

Example: Consider a person navigating a demanding job with long hours and high-pressure deadlines. The persistent stress from work-related challenges can contribute to sustained high blood pressure, potentially impacting their cardiovascular health.

Immune System Dysfunction: Prolonged stress weakens the immune system, making individuals more susceptible to infections and illnesses. The immune response becomes compromised, and the body's ability to fend off pathogens diminishes.

Example: Picture a student enduring a stressful exam period. The pressure and anxiety may compromise their immune function, leading to increased susceptibility to colds or other infections during this taxing time.

Digestive Issues: Stress has a significant impact on the digestive system. It can lead to conditions such as irritable bowel syndrome (IBS), acid reflux, and inflammation in the gut. The intricate network between the brain and the digestive system, known as the gut-brain axis, becomes disrupted under chronic stress.

Example: Imagine an individual facing ongoing work-related stress. This stress may manifest in gastrointestinal discomfort, with symptoms such as stomachaches or indigestion becoming a frequent occurrence.

Muscle Tension and Pain: Chronic stress often manifests in physical symptoms, including muscle tension and pain. The body's natural response to stress involves preparing for physical exertion, leading to the tightening of muscles. When this tension persists, it can result in chronic pain conditions.

Example: A person dealing with ongoing family-related stress may experience persistent tension in their shoulders and neck, potentially leading to chronic pain and discomfort.

Cognitive and Emotional Impact:

Cognitive Impairment: Chronic stress has notable effects on cognitive function. It can impair memory, concentration, and decision-making abilities. The sustained release of stress hormones can negatively impact the hippocampus, a region of the brain crucial for memory and learning.

Example: Consider a professional managing the stress of a demanding job. The continuous pressure may contribute to difficulty concentrating, impacting their ability to perform tasks effectively.

Mental Health Challenges: Prolonged stress is a significant contributor to mental health challenges, including anxiety and depression. The constant activation of the stress response can disrupt neurotransmitter balance in the brain, influencing mood regulation.

Example: Imagine a caregiver facing the daily stressors of tending to a loved one with a chronic illness. The emotional toll of caregiving may contribute to feelings of anxiety or depression over time.

Sleep Disturbances: Stress often disrupts the sleep-wake cycle, leading to difficulties in falling asleep or staying asleep. The heightened state of alertness associated with chronic stress can interfere with the natural rhythms of the sleep process.

Example: Think of a student preparing for a critical examination. The stress and anxiety surrounding the exams may lead to frequent sleep disturbances, impacting their overall sleep quality and contributing to fatigue.

Impact on Emotional Well-Being:

Heightened Emotional Reactivity: Chronic stress can lead to heightened emotional reactivity, making individuals more prone to intense emotional responses to everyday challenges. This heightened reactivity can strain relationships and contribute to emotional exhaustion.

Example: Consider a parent juggling the responsibilities of work and family. The persistent stress may result in increased irritability and emotional sensitivity, affecting interactions with family members.

Reduced Resilience: Chronic stress diminishes emotional resilience—the ability to bounce back from challenges. Individuals experiencing ongoing stress may find it challenging to cope with setbacks, leading to a sense of helplessness.

Example: Picture an individual navigating the stress of a tumultuous relationship. The emotional toll may erode their resilience, making it challenging to cope with subsequent challenges in other areas of life.

Social Withdrawal: The impact of stress often extends to social dynamics. Individuals facing chronic stress may withdraw from social interactions, experiencing a sense of isolation and loneliness.

Example: Think of an individual grappling with work-related stress. The demands of the job may lead to social withdrawal, as they find it challenging to engage in social activities or maintain connections with friends.

Breaking the Cycle with The Art of Relaxation:

Understanding the far-reaching impact of stress on well-being is the first step toward reclaiming inner harmony. "The Art of Relaxation" serves as a guide to navigate this tumultuous terrain, offering practical strategies and mindful practices to counteract the detrimental effects of chronic stress. By cultivating intentional relaxation, individuals embark on a transformative journey toward holistic well-being—a journey that harmonizes the body, mind, and spirit in the pursuit of inner tranquility.

Understanding Stress

Unraveling the Intricacies of a Modern Nemesis

In the bustling tapestry of contemporary life, stress emerges as a ubiquitous companion, intricately woven into the fabric of our daily experiences. Yet, the concept of stress is far from simple; it is a nuanced interplay of physiological responses, psychological perceptions, and the ever-evolving dynamics of the modern world. As we embark on the exploration of "The Art of Relaxation," understanding stress becomes a crucial first step in unraveling the complexities of this modern nemesis.

The Nature of Stress:

At its essence, stress is the body's natural response to any demand or challenge. Whether it be a looming deadline, a sudden change, or an unexpected event, the body gears up to meet the perceived threat, preparing for a "fight or flight" response. This physiological reaction is deeply ingrained in our evolutionary history, a mechanism designed to enhance survival in the face of immediate danger.

While this acute stress response is vital for navigating immediate threats, the challenges of the modern world often introduce a different dynamic—chronic stress. Unlike the brief spikes of stress associated with survival situations, chronic stress is characterized by prolonged activation of the stress response, contributing to a myriad of physical, mental, and emotional implications.

The Stress Response:

Fight or Flight: When the brain perceives a threat, it triggers the release of stress hormones, including adrenaline and cortisol. This mobilizes the body's resources, redirecting energy to vital functions such as the heart, lungs, and muscles—preparing the individual for immediate action.

The Role of the Amygdala: The amygdala, a region in the brain responsible for processing emotions, plays a pivotal role in the stress response. It acts as a sentinel, swiftly identifying potential threats and activating the stress response cascade.

The HPA Axis: The hypothalamus-pituitary-adrenal (HPA) axis is a key player in the stress response. The hypothalamus signals the pituitary gland to release adrenocorticotropic hormone (ACTH), which, in turn, stimulates the adrenal glands to produce cortisol. Cortisol, often referred to as the "stress hormone," helps regulate various physiological processes.

The Physiological Impact: The stress response triggers a cascade of physiological changes—increased heart rate, heightened alertness, and redirected blood flow. These changes are adaptive in the short term but can become detrimental when activated persistently.

Types of Stress:

Acute Stress: This is the most common form of stress, typically resulting from immediate challenges or demands. Examples include a tight deadline at work, a sudden traffic jam, or a minor disagreement.

Chronic Stress: Chronic stress is characterized by prolonged exposure to stressors, often related to ongoing life circumstances. Examples include financial strain, long-term caregiving responsibilities, or persistently challenging work environments.

Eustress: Eustress, often referred to as "good stress," is the positive form of stress associated with exciting or challenging events. While it can be invigorating, it still activates the stress response.

Perception and Appraisal:

Crucial to understanding stress is the role of perception and appraisal. How an individual perceives and appraises a situation influences whether it is deemed stressful. What one person may find exhilarating, another might perceive as overwhelming. This subjectivity underscores the importance of individual differences and coping mechanisms in the stress response.

The Impact of Modern Lifestyles:

The dynamics of modern living have ushered in a new era of stressors. Technological advances, societal expectations, and the relentless pace of life contribute to an environment where chronic stress has become pervasive. The perpetual connectivity of the digital age, for instance, introduces constant stimuli, blurring the lines between work and personal life.

Individual Responses to Stress:

Coping Mechanisms: Individuals employ various coping mechanisms to manage stress. Some turn to exercise, mindfulness, or social support, while others may resort to unhealthy coping strategies such as overeating, substance use, or withdrawal.

Individual Resilience: Resilience plays a crucial role in how individuals navigate stress. Resilient individuals demonstrate an ability to bounce back from challenges, adapting to adversity and maintaining psychological well-being.

The Interconnected Impact:

Stress doesn't exist in isolation; it permeates every aspect of an individual's life. Chronic stress can contribute to a cascade of physical health issues, including cardiovascular problems, gastrointestinal disturbances, and compromised immune function. It also influences mental health, contributing to conditions such as anxiety, depression, and burnout.

Breaking the Stress Cycle: The Role of Relaxation:

Understanding stress is the first step toward breaking the cycle. "The Art of Relaxation" serves as a guide to empower individuals to navigate the intricate landscape of stress with intentionality and mindfulness. By cultivating practices that promote relaxation and resilience, individuals can mitigate the impact of chronic stress, fostering a path toward holistic well-being.

In the chapters that follow, we delve into the artful practices that counteract the detrimental effects of stress, offering a transformative journey toward inner harmony and balance. Through intentional relaxation, individuals can reclaim agency over their stress responses, cultivating a life marked by tranquility, resilience, and a profound

The Science of Stress: Decoding the Intricacies of the Body's Response

Stress is not merely a psychological state; it is a complex physiological response intricately woven into the fabric of human biology. Understanding the science of stress involves delving into the intricate mechanisms that orchestrate the body's reaction to perceived threats, unveiling a symphony of hormones, neural signals, and adaptive responses.

At the heart of the stress response is the brain's sentinel—the amygdala. This almond-shaped structure, nestled deep within the brain's temporal lobe, acts as the rapid-response center for emotional processing. When the amygdala perceives a potential threat, it sets off a chain reaction, triggering the hypothalamus to signal the release of stress hormones.

The hypothalamus, a crucial regulator of bodily functions, communicates with the pituitary gland to release adrenocorticotropic hormone (ACTH). This hormone, in turn, stimulates the adrenal glands, located atop the kidneys, to produce cortisol—a central player in the stress response.

Cortisol, often referred to as the "stress hormone," serves a multitude of functions. It mobilizes energy reserves, sharpens the senses, and redirects blood flow to critical systems such as the muscles and the heart. In essence, cortisol prepares the body for action, whether it be confronting a physical threat or navigating a challenging situation.

While this acute stress response is adaptive in the short term, chronic activation of the stress system can lead to a cascade of physiological changes. Prolonged exposure to elevated cortisol levels has been linked to a range of health issues, including cardiovascular problems, impaired immune function, and disruptions in metabolic processes.

Moreover, chronic stress can influence the intricate interplay between the brain and the immune system. The field of psychoneuroimmunology explores how emotional and psychological factors, including stress, impact the body's immune response. Elevated stress levels have been associated with increased susceptibility to infections, slower wound healing, and a heightened risk of autoimmune disorders.

Understanding the science of stress goes beyond recognizing its psychological impact; it unveils a sophisticated network of physiological responses designed to enhance survival. As we navigate the complexities of modern life, decoding this science becomes pivotal in developing strategies to mitigate the detrimental effects of chronic stress. "The Art of Relaxation" serves as a guide in this endeavor, offering insights and practices to recalibrate the body's stress response and foster a state of balance and well-being.

Identifying Personal Stressors: Unraveling the Threads of Individual Strain

In the journey toward well-being, the ability to identify personal stressors stands as a crucial cornerstone. Personal stressors are unique to each individual, stemming from a myriad of factors that contribute to the complex tapestry of daily life. Unraveling these threads of stress requires a mindful exploration of one's experiences, reactions, and the various facets that weave into the intricate fabric of personal stress.

Reflecting on Life Domains:

Personal stressors often manifest across different domains of life. Work, relationships, health, and personal aspirations all contribute to the intricate dance of stressors. Reflecting on each domain provides valuable insights into the specific areas that may be sources of strain.

Work-related Stressors:

Consider the demands of your professional life. Are tight deadlines, a heavy workload, or challenging interpersonal dynamics causing stress? Identifying specific stressors in the workplace allows for targeted strategies to manage and alleviate the pressure.

Example: A project manager may experience stress due to the pressure of meeting tight project deadlines or navigating team conflicts.

Relationship-based Stressors:

Personal relationships can be a wellspring of joy, but they also introduce unique stressors. Reflect on dynamics with family, friends, or romantic partners. Are communication challenges, conflicts, or unmet expectations contributing to stress?

Example: A parent might identify stressors related to balancing the needs of children, managing household responsibilities, or navigating disagreements with a partner.

Health-related Stressors:

Physical health and well-being play a significant role in overall stress levels. Chronic illnesses, lifestyle factors, or concerns about one's health can contribute to stress. Understanding how health intersects with stress allows for proactive self-care.

Example: An individual managing a chronic condition may experience stress related to treatment plans, symptom management, or concerns about long-term health outcomes.

Personal Aspirations and Goals:

Ambitions and aspirations can fuel motivation, but they can also introduce stressors. Reflect on personal goals and the expectations placed on oneself. Are unrealistic expectations, fear of failure, or a lack of work-life balance contributing to stress?

Example: A student working towards academic excellence may grapple with stressors related to perfectionism, fear of academic failure, or the pressure to meet external expectations.

External Stressors:

Beyond personal realms, external factors such as societal pressures, financial concerns, or global events can impact stress levels. Recognizing the influence of external stressors provides context to individual experiences.

Example: Economic uncertainties, political unrest, or environmental changes may introduce external stressors that individuals need to navigate.

Mindful Self-Reflection:

Identifying personal stressors requires a practice of mindful self-reflection. This involves introspection, journaling, or engaging in conversations with trusted confidants. By observing emotional responses, physical sensations, and patterns of thought during various situations, individuals can gain valuable insights into their unique stress triggers.

Cultivating Awareness:

Awareness is the compass that guides the navigation of personal stressors. As individuals cultivate a heightened awareness of their experiences, they gain the capacity to respond intentionally. This awareness empowers proactive stress management strategies, fostering a more balanced and resilient approach to life's challenges.

The Role of "The Art of Relaxation":

"The Art of Relaxation" serves as a companion in this journey of self-discovery. It provides tools, practices, and insights to navigate personal stressors with mindfulness and intentionality. By identifying and understanding these stressors, individuals embark on a transformative path toward cultivating resilience, balance, and a deeper sense of well-being.

The Mind-Body Connection

A Harmonious Symphony of Well-Being

The mind and body, often perceived as distinct entities, are inextricably linked in a profound and intricate dance—a symphony of interconnectedness that shapes our experiences, perceptions, and overall well-being. Understanding the mind-body connection goes beyond recognizing their coexistence; it unveils the dynamic interplay that influences physical health, emotional states, and the very essence of human experience.

The Science of Connection:

At the heart of the mind-body connection lies a complex network of communication pathways between the brain, the central nervous system, and various bodily systems. This communication occurs through neurotransmitters, hormones, and intricate feedback loops, creating a continuous dialogue between mental and physical states.

The brain, acting as the command center, interprets thoughts, emotions, and external stimuli, sending signals that elicit physiological responses throughout the body. For instance, the experience of stress triggers the release of stress hormones, impacting heart rate, blood pressure, and immune function.

Impact on Physical Health:

The influence of the mind on physical health is profound. Consider the placebo effect, where individuals experience real physiological changes solely based on their belief in the efficacy of a treatment. This phenomenon underscores the mind's ability to influence the body's healing mechanisms.

Stress and the Immune System: Chronic stress, often rooted in psychological factors, can compromise the immune system. The release of stress hormones like cortisol can suppress immune function, making individuals more susceptible to infections and illnesses.

Emotions and Heart Health: Emotional well-being is closely tied to cardiovascular health. Positive emotions, such as joy and gratitude, have been associated with improved heart health, while chronic negative emotions can contribute to the development of cardiovascular conditions.

Pain Perception: The mind-body connection also plays a role in pain perception. The brain's interpretation of pain signals can be influenced by emotional states, stress levels, and cognitive processes. Mind-body practices like mindfulness have demonstrated efficacy in managing chronic pain.

Emotional Impact:

Emotions, often considered products of the mind, have tangible effects on the body. The expression of joy, sadness, anger, or fear is not confined to the realm of feelings; it manifests physiologically.

The Stress-Emotion Loop: Stressful emotions trigger the release of stress hormones, contributing to the body's stress response. Conversely, chronic stress can lead to persistent negative emotions, creating a feedback loop that perpetuates both mental and physical distress.

Mood and Hormonal Balance: Hormones, the body's chemical messengers, play a crucial role in regulating mood. Imbalances in hormones, influenced by factors such as stress, can contribute to mood disorders like anxiety and depression.

Gut-Brain Axis: The gut, often referred to as the "second brain," communicates bidirectionally with the central nervous system. Emotional states can impact gut function, and conversely, gut health can influence mood and emotional well-being.

Mind-Body Practices:

Recognizing the profound interconnection between the mind and body has given rise to mind-body practices—approaches that leverage this connection to enhance overall well-being.

Mindfulness and Meditation: These practices involve cultivating present-moment awareness and redirecting the focus of the mind. Research has shown that mindfulness and meditation can reduce stress, improve mood, and positively impact physical health.

Yoga: Beyond its physical postures, yoga integrates breath control and mindfulness, promoting a harmonious union of the mind and body. Regular practice has been associated with reduced stress, increased flexibility, and enhanced emotional well-being.

Biofeedback: This technique involves monitoring physiological functions such as heart rate or muscle tension and providing real-time feedback. Individuals can learn to consciously influence these functions, promoting relaxation and stress reduction.

Breathwork: Conscious control of breathing patterns can influence the autonomic nervous system, impacting stress levels and emotional states. Techniques like diaphragmatic breathing are used to induce a relaxation response.

Psychoneuroimmunology:

Psychoneuroimmunology explores the bidirectional communication between the mind, nervous system, and immune system. Research in this field has demonstrated the impact of psychological factors on immune function, highlighting the holistic nature of well-being.

Cultivating Mind-Body Harmony:

The cultivation of mind-body harmony involves intentional practices that foster balance, awareness, and resilience.

Holistic Health Practices: Adopting a holistic approach to health considers the interconnectedness of physical, mental, and emotional well-being. This includes a balanced diet, regular exercise, and sufficient rest.

Emotional Intelligence: Cultivating emotional intelligence involves recognizing and managing one's own emotions and understanding their impact on physical health. This self-awareness contributes to overall well-being.

Positive Lifestyle Choices: Engaging in activities that bring joy, practicing gratitude, and fostering positive social connections contribute to a positive mind-body environment.

Therapeutic Approaches: Integrative approaches to healthcare, combining conventional and complementary therapies, acknowledge the mind-body connection. These may include approaches like acupuncture, massage therapy, or cognitive-behavioral therapy.

In essence, understanding the mind-body connection is an invitation to explore the profound implications of our thoughts, emotions, and actions on our physical health and vice versa. It is a recognition of the intricate dance that shapes our experiences and an empowerment to consciously navigate this symbiotic relationship in the pursuit of holistic well-being. As we embrace this awareness, we embark on a journey toward a harmonious symphony of mind and body—a journey enriched by practices that honor the interconnected nature of our human experience.

Exploring the Mind-Body Relationship: Navigating the Intricate Interplay of Well-Being

The mind and body, two seemingly distinct realms, are intimately entwined in a profound and dynamic relationship—a relationship that forms the essence of our human experience. Exploring the mind-body relationship unveils the intricacies of how thoughts, emotions, and physical well-being intersect, shaping the tapestry of our lives in profound ways.

The Mind as Architect:

The mind, often regarded as the architect of our reality, is the epicenter of thoughts, beliefs, and emotions. It processes experiences, interprets stimuli, and constructs the narrative through which we perceive the world. This mental landscape is not confined to the brain alone; it extends its influence to every cell and system within the body.

The Language of Neurotransmitters:

Within the brain, neurotransmitters act as messengers, transmitting signals that bridge the communication between neurons. Serotonin, dopamine, and norepinephrine, among others, play pivotal roles in regulating mood, motivation, and overall mental well-being. The delicate balance of these neurotransmitters shapes emotional states and influences the body's physiological responses.

Emotions as Physiological Symphony:

Emotions, the intricate dance of joy, sorrow, anger, and fear, are not confined to the realm of feelings; they resonate throughout the body. The experience of joy, for instance, may manifest in the release of endorphins, the body's natural feel-good chemicals. Conversely, chronic stress or anxiety can trigger the release of cortisol and adrenaline, impacting heart rate, immune function, and digestive processes.

The Physical Manifestation of Stress:

Stress, a ubiquitous companion in modern life, epitomizes the mind-body relationship. When the mind perceives a threat, whether real or imagined, it signals the body's stress response. This activation involves the release of stress hormones, preparing the body for "fight or flight." The physiological manifestations of stress, such as increased heart rate, shallow breathing, and muscle tension, reflect the intricate dialogue between mind and body.

Mind-Body Practices as Bridges:

Mind-body practices serve as bridges that consciously connect and harmonize the realms of mental and physical well-being. These practices acknowledge the inseparable nature of the mind and body, offering transformative tools to enhance overall health.

Mindfulness Meditation: Rooted in ancient contemplative traditions, mindfulness meditation invites individuals to cultivate present-moment awareness. By anchoring attention to the breath or sensations, individuals foster a deep connection between mind and body, promoting relaxation and stress reduction.

Yoga: More than a physical exercise, yoga unifies breath, movement, and mindfulness. The postures (asanas) serve as gateways to attuning the mind to bodily sensations, fostering flexibility not only in the body but also in the mind.

Breathwork: Conscious control of breath serves as a potent modulator of the autonomic nervous system. Techniques like diaphragmatic breathing or alternate nostril breathing influence the mind's state and, in turn, impact physiological responses.

Biofeedback: This practice involves monitoring physiological functions such as heart rate or muscle tension and providing real-time feedback. Individuals learn to consciously influence these functions, promoting relaxation and stress reduction.

The Gut-Brain Connection:

Beyond the traditional understanding of the mind-body relationship, recent research has highlighted the significance of the gut-brain connection. The enteric nervous system, often referred to as the "second brain," communicates bidirectionally with the central nervous system. This intricate network influences not only digestive processes but also emotional well-being.

Psychoneuroimmunology:

The field of psychoneuroimmunology explores the interplay between psychological factors, the nervous system, and the immune system. It underscores how mental states can influence immune function, emphasizing the holistic nature of well-being.

Cognitive-Behavioral Influence:

Cognitive-behavioral approaches recognize the power of thoughts in shaping emotional and physical responses. By restructuring negative thought patterns, individuals can influence their emotional states and, subsequently, their physiological well-being.

Embracing Holistic Health:

Exploring the mind-body relationship invites us to embrace a holistic understanding of health—one that recognizes the interconnected nature of physical, mental, and emotional well-being. Holistic health practices encompass balanced nutrition, regular exercise, sufficient rest, and intentional self-care, acknowledging that these factors collectively contribute to overall vitality.

A Symphony of Well-Being:

In the grand symphony of well-being, the mind and body coalesce as instruments, each contributing to the harmonious composition of our lives. Exploring this relationship is an ongoing journey of self-discovery, mindfulness, and intentional practices that honor the intricate interplay between mental and physical states. As we navigate this exploration, we cultivate a profound awareness—one that enriches our understanding of self and empowers us to orchestrate a life marked by balance, resilience, and a deep sense of interconnected wholeness.

Practices for Harmonizing Mind and Body: Cultivating Wholeness and Well-Being

In the quest for holistic well-being, the harmonization of mind and body stands as a transformative journey—one that invites individuals to explore practices that nurture the intricate interplay between mental and physical states. These practices, rooted in ancient wisdom and supported by contemporary research, serve as pathways to cultivate a sense of wholeness, balance, and overall vitality.

1. Mindfulness Meditation:

At the heart of mind-body harmonization lies mindfulness meditation, a practice that invites individuals to cultivate present-moment awareness. Rooted in contemplative traditions, mindfulness involves directing attention to the breath, bodily sensations, or the unfolding moment without judgment. By anchoring the mind in the present, individuals forge a deep connection with bodily sensations, fostering relaxation and mental clarity.

Research highlights the myriad benefits of mindfulness, including stress reduction, improved emotional well-being, and changes in brain structure associated with enhanced self-awareness. Integrating mindfulness into daily life serves as a cornerstone for harmonizing the mind and body, offering a refuge of stillness amid the tumult of modern living.

2. Yoga:

Yoga, an ancient practice with roots in India, embodies the integration of breath, movement, and mindfulness. Beyond physical postures, or asanas, yoga encompasses a holistic approach to well-being. Each posture becomes a gateway to attuning the mind to bodily sensations, fostering flexibility not only in the body but also in the mind.

The marriage of movement and breath in yoga stimulates the parasympathetic nervous system, promoting relaxation. Regular practice has been associated with increased flexibility, improved mood, and enhanced overall vitality. Whether through gentle restorative practices or dynamic vinyasa flows, yoga serves as a profound vehicle for harmonizing the mind-body relationship.

3. Breathwork:

Conscious control of the breath emerges as a potent tool for mind-body harmonization. Various breathwork techniques, such as diaphragmatic breathing or alternate nostril breathing, influence the autonomic nervous system, bridging the gap between conscious and subconscious processes.

Deep, intentional breaths activate the parasympathetic nervous system, inducing a relaxation response. The rhythmic cadence of breath becomes a bridge, aligning mental states with physiological well-being. Regular breathwork practices empower individuals to modulate stress, reduce anxiety, and foster a sense of calm within the body and mind.

4. Biofeedback:

In the realm of mind-body practices, biofeedback serves as a bridge between conscious awareness and physiological responses. This technique involves monitoring physiological functions, such as heart rate variability or muscle tension, and providing real-time feedback. Through this feedback loop, individuals gain insight into their body's responses and learn to consciously influence these functions.

Biofeedback has proven effective in stress reduction, pain management, and improving overall emotional well-being. By fostering awareness of bodily processes, individuals develop a heightened sense of agency over their physiological responses, contributing to the harmonization of the mind and body.

5. Cognitive-Behavioral Techniques:

Cognitive-behavioral approaches recognize the influence of thoughts on emotional and physical states. By identifying and restructuring negative thought patterns, individuals can positively impact their mental and physical well-being. These techniques involve challenging distorted thinking, cultivating positive affirmations, and fostering a mindset that supports overall health.

Research indicates the efficacy of cognitive-behavioral techniques in managing conditions such as anxiety, depression, and chronic pain. By harmonizing thought patterns with bodily responses, individuals embark on a journey of holistic well-being.

6. Movement Practices:

Beyond structured forms like yoga, incorporating mindful movement into daily life contributes to mind-body harmonization. Tai Chi and Qigong, ancient Chinese practices, involve intentional, flowing movements synchronized with breath and mindfulness. These practices promote balance, flexibility, and a sense of centeredness, fostering harmony between mind and body.

Regular physical activity, whether through walking, dancing, or engaging in sports, releases endorphins—natural mood-enhancing chemicals. The integration of movement into daily routines becomes a celebration of the body's capabilities and a nurturing practice for holistic well-being.

7. Nutrition and Mindful Eating:

The choices we make in nourishing our bodies profoundly influence both mental and physical states. Mindful eating, an awareness-centered approach to consuming food, involves savoring each bite, recognizing hunger and fullness cues, and cultivating a non-judgmental relationship with food.

Balanced nutrition supports cognitive function, mood regulation, and overall vitality. By mindfully attending to the nourishment of the body, individuals contribute to the harmonization of mental and physical well-being.

8. Nature Connection:

Engaging with nature becomes a soul-nourishing practice that harmonizes the mind and body. Whether through forest bathing, spending time in green spaces, or connecting with natural elements, this practice aligns individuals with the rhythmic cycles of the earth.

Research suggests that exposure to nature reduces stress, enhances mood, and promotes overall well-being. Nature becomes a sanctuary for recalibrating the mind and rejuvenating the body.

Conclusion:

Harmonizing the mind and body is not a destination but an ongoing journey—one that involves intentional practices, self-reflection, and a deepening understanding of the interconnected nature of our being. These practices, whether ancient or contemporary, serve as invitations to explore the richness of the mind-body relationship. As individuals embark on this transformative journey, they cultivate a profound sense of wholeness, resilience, and an empowered alignment with the symphony of life.

The Power of Breath

Unveiling the Essence of Life and Well-Being

In the rhythmic dance of life, the breath stands as an unassuming yet profound force—the silent conductor orchestrating the symphony of our existence. Beyond its physiological role of oxygenating the body, the breath holds transformative power, serving as a gateway to enhanced well-being, mindfulness, and a harmonious connection between mind and body.

Breath as Life Force:

The breath, often referred to as prana in ancient yogic traditions, is more than a mere biological function; it is the very essence of life. With each inhalation, life-giving oxygen enters the body, fueling cellular processes and vitalizing every organ. Each exhalation releases carbon dioxide, the byproduct of metabolism, completing a cycle that sustains life itself.

Recognizing the breath as a sacred life force invites a shift in perception. The act of breathing becomes a conscious communion with the energy that animates us, fostering a deep appreciation for the interconnected nature of all living things.

Conscious Breathing and Mindfulness:

The breath serves as a perennial anchor to the present moment. Conscious breathing, a cornerstone of mindfulness practices, involves directing focused attention to the inhalation and exhalation. This intentional awareness of the breath becomes a doorway to the present, transcending the pull of past regrets or future anxieties.

Mindful breathing offers a refuge from the incessant chatter of the mind. As individuals consciously inhale and exhale, they cultivate a state of heightened awareness—a state where thoughts arise and dissipate like passing clouds, leaving a serene canvas of present-moment experience.

Regulating the Nervous System:

The breath is intricately connected to the autonomic nervous system, the regulator of involuntary bodily functions. Deliberate modulation of the breath can influence the balance between the sympathetic (fight or flight) and parasympathetic (rest and digest) branches of the nervous system.

Slow, deep breaths activate the parasympathetic nervous system, inducing a relaxation response. This physiological shift results in reduced heart rate, lowered blood pressure, and a sense of calm. By consciously regulating the breath, individuals can navigate stress and cultivate a state of inner tranquility.

Stress Reduction and Emotional Well-Being:

The breath emerges as a powerful ally in the face of stress and emotional turbulence. Stress often triggers shallow, rapid breathing—a survival response that prepares the body for immediate action. However, chronic stress can perpetuate this pattern, contributing to heightened anxiety and diminished well-being.

Conscious breathwork, such as diaphragmatic breathing or counted breath cycles, interrupts the stress response. It creates space for intentional, slow breaths that signal the body to shift from a state of tension to one of relaxation. This intentional modulation of the breath becomes a practical tool for managing stress and promoting emotional balance.

Breathwork Techniques:

Numerous breathwork techniques, rooted in ancient traditions and contemporary practices, harness the transformative power of the breath. These techniques offer individuals a diverse array of tools to explore and integrate into their well-being routines.

- Diaphragmatic Breathing: This technique involves deep inhalations that engage the diaphragm, allowing the abdomen to expand. Diaphragmatic breathing promotes relaxation and optimal oxygen exchange.

- Box Breathing: Also known as square breathing, this technique involves inhaling, holding the breath, exhaling, and holding again—all for equal counts. It fosters balance, focus, and a sense of centeredness.

- Alternate Nostril Breathing (Nadi Shodhana): A yogic technique, alternate nostril breathing involves inhaling and exhaling through one nostril at a time. This practice is believed to balance energy channels and promote mental clarity.

- 4-7-8 Breathing: This technique, popularized by Dr. Andrew Weil, involves inhaling for a count of 4, holding the breath for 7 counts, and exhaling for 8 counts. It induces a deep sense of relaxation and can be used as a sleep aid.

- Breath Awareness Meditation: Simply observing the natural flow of the breath without attempting to control it is a foundational mindfulness meditation practice. This form of meditation cultivates present-moment awareness and a deep connection with the breath.

Integration into Daily Life:

The power of breath extends beyond designated practice sessions; it is a constant companion in the ebb and flow of daily life. Integrating conscious breathing into routine activities—whether walking, working, or taking moments of intentional pause—infuses each moment with mindfulness and presence.

By weaving conscious breathing into the fabric of daily existence, individuals foster resilience, emotional well-being, and a harmonious connection between mind and body. The breath becomes a guide—a reminder of the profound simplicity that resides within us, offering solace, clarity, and a continuous pathway to the essence of life itself.

Breathing Techniques for Stress Reduction: Unveiling the Calming Power Within

In the fast-paced rhythm of modern life, stress often becomes a constant companion, impacting both mental and physical well-being. Amid the chaos, the breath emerges as a potent ally, offering accessible and effective techniques for stress reduction. These breathing practices, rooted in ancient wisdom and validated by contemporary research, unveil the calming power within, providing individuals with practical tools to navigate stress and cultivate a sense of inner tranquility.

Diaphragmatic Breathing:

One of the simplest yet most impactful techniques, diaphragmatic breathing involves engaging the diaphragm to facilitate deep, abdominal breaths. By consciously inhaling through the nose, allowing the diaphragm to descend, and exhaling slowly through pursed lips, individuals activate the relaxation response. Diaphragmatic breathing not only reduces stress but also promotes optimal oxygen exchange, fostering a sense of calm and centeredness.

Box Breathing (Four-Square Breathing):

Box breathing is a structured technique that creates a rhythmic pattern of inhalation, holding the breath, exhalation, and another breath hold—all for equal counts. For example, inhale for a count of four, hold for four, exhale for four, and hold for four. This method not only provides a clear structure for breath regulation but also brings balance to the autonomic nervous system, promoting relaxation and mental clarity.

4-7-8 Breathing:

Introduced by Dr. Andrew Weil, the 4-7-8 breathing technique involves inhaling for a count of four, holding the breath for seven, and exhaling for a count of eight. This practice leverages the principles of deep breathing and extended exhalation, triggering the parasympathetic nervous system's relaxation response. It is particularly effective as a quick stress-relief tool and a prelude to restful sleep.

Alternate Nostril Breathing (Nadi Shodhana):

Rooted in yogic traditions, alternate nostril breathing is a technique that balances the flow of energy in the body. By alternating between inhaling and exhaling through each nostril, individuals aim to harmonize the left and right hemispheres of the brain. This practice not only reduces stress but also enhances focus and mental clarity.

Breath Awareness Meditation:

A foundational mindfulness practice, breath awareness meditation involves observing the natural flow of the breath without attempting to control it. By directing attention to the sensation of breath entering and leaving the body, individuals cultivate present-moment awareness. This form of meditation provides a sanctuary of stillness amidst the chaos, promoting a grounded and centered state of being.

Integration into Daily Life:

The beauty of these breathing techniques lies in their adaptability to daily life. Whether incorporated during moments of stress, integrated into a morning routine, or practiced as intentional breaks throughout the day, these techniques offer a continuous thread of calmness.

Conclusion:

The breath, a constant and accessible companion, serves as a gateway to stress reduction and enhanced well-being. These breathing techniques, each a unique expression of the profound connection between breath and relaxation, empower individuals to reclaim a sense of calm amidst the whirlwind of daily challenges. As individuals embrace the simplicity and effectiveness of these practices, they unlock the transformative potential of the breath—the silent guide to tranquility within.

Mindful Breathing in Everyday Life: Cultivating Presence and Tranquility

In the hustle and bustle of daily life, where demands and distractions abound, the practice of mindful breathing emerges as a transformative tool for cultivating presence, reducing stress, and fostering a sense of tranquility. Grounded in ancient contemplative traditions, mindful breathing invites individuals to bring conscious awareness to the simple yet profound act of breathing, making each breath an opportunity for connection and rejuvenation.

1. Commuting Mindfully:

Whether stuck in traffic or navigating public transportation, the daily commute often becomes a source of stress. Mindful breathing provides a sanctuary within the chaos. As you wait for the traffic light to change or stand in a crowded subway car, take a moment to center yourself by focusing on the rhythm of your breath. Inhale deeply through the nose, feeling the expansion of your chest and abdomen, and exhale slowly through pursed lips. This mindful pause amidst the commute can transform the experience from stressful to contemplative.

2. Mindful Breaks at Work:

In the midst of a busy workday, brief moments of mindful breathing offer a reset for the mind and body. Set a reminder to take short breaks, step away from the desk, and find a quiet space. Close your eyes and bring attention to your breath. Notice the sensation of each inhalation and exhalation. This mini-meditation not only refreshes the mind but also enhances focus and productivity.

3. Mindful Eating:

Mealtime provides a natural opportunity for incorporating mindful breathing. Before taking the first bite, take a moment to appreciate the nourishment in front of you. Inhale the aroma, exhale slowly, and savor each mouthful. Mindful breathing during meals not only fosters a deeper connection with the act of eating but also supports digestion and a more conscious relationship with food.

4. Dealing with Stressful Situations:

When faced with stress or challenging situations, mindful breathing becomes an anchor to navigate the turbulence. Instead of reacting impulsively, pause and take a few conscious breaths. Inhale calmness, exhale tension. This intentional breathwork creates space for thoughtful responses, promoting emotional regulation and resilience in the face of stress.

5. Connecting with Nature:

Mindful breathing can deepen the connection with nature, whether you're taking a stroll in the park or simply stepping outside. As you inhale the fresh air, let your breath become attuned to the natural rhythms around you. The gentle sway of leaves, the rustle of branches, or the rhythmic sounds of waves can harmonize with your breath, creating a serene symphony of mindfulness.

Conclusion:

Mindful breathing in everyday life is not a separate practice but an integrated approach to living with presence and intention. By infusing conscious awareness into routine moments, individuals tap into the transformative power of the breath. Each inhale becomes an opportunity for grounding, and each exhale becomes a release of tension. As mindful breathing becomes woven into the fabric of daily experiences, it shapes a life marked by tranquility, awareness, and a profound connection with the present moment.

Mindfulness Meditation

A Journey into Present-Moment Awareness

In a world often characterized by relentless pace and constant stimuli, mindfulness meditation emerges as a timeless practice—a profound journey into the essence of present-moment awareness. Rooted in ancient contemplative traditions, mindfulness meditation has transcended cultural boundaries to become a widely embraced pathway to mental well-being, stress reduction, and a deeper understanding of the self.

Defining Mindfulness Meditation:

At its core, mindfulness meditation is a practice that invites individuals to cultivate a heightened state of awareness by directing focused attention to the present moment. It involves intentionally paying attention to thoughts, sensations, and emotions without judgment. The essence lies in observing the flow of experience with a non-reactive and compassionate mindset.

Fundamental Elements of Mindfulness Meditation:

Breath as an Anchor:

Central to mindfulness meditation is the breath—an ever-present and accessible anchor to the present moment. Practitioners often begin by focusing on the sensation of breathing, feeling the rise and fall of the chest or the flow of air through the nostrils. The breath serves as a grounding point, providing a focal point for attention.

Non-Judgmental Awareness:

Mindfulness encourages an attitude of non-judgmental observation. Rather than evaluating thoughts or sensations as good or bad, practitioners aim to witness them with acceptance. This non-judgmental awareness extends to the entirety of the present experience, creating a space for the unfolding of thoughts and emotions without attachment.

Body Scan and Sensory Awareness:

Mindfulness meditation often involves a body scan, where attention is systematically directed to different parts of the body. This practice fosters a deep connection with bodily sensations and enhances awareness of physical experiences. Sensory awareness extends beyond the body to encompass sounds, smells, and the overall environment.

Cultivating Equanimity:

Equanimity, a sense of calmness and balance in the face of various experiences, is a key aspect of mindfulness meditation. Practitioners learn to observe the fluctuations of the mind with equanimity, recognizing that thoughts and emotions are transient and do not define the self. This cultivated equanimity contributes to emotional resilience and a more harmonious relationship with the ups and downs of life.

Mindful Movement and Activities:

While sitting meditation is a foundational practice, mindfulness extends to movement and daily activities. Mindful walking, eating, and engaging in routine tasks become opportunities for integrating present-moment awareness. The intention is to bring the same focused attention and non-judgmental awareness to every aspect of life.

Scientific Validation:

The effectiveness of mindfulness meditation is not confined to contemplative traditions; it has garnered significant attention in scientific research. Studies suggest that regular mindfulness practice can lead to positive changes in the brain, impacting areas associated with attention, emotional regulation, and self-awareness. Furthermore, mindfulness-based interventions have been incorporated into therapeutic approaches for stress reduction, anxiety, and depression.

Applications Beyond Meditation Cushions:

Mindfulness meditation is not restricted to formal sitting sessions. Its principles are increasingly applied in various settings, including schools, workplaces, and clinical settings. Mindfulness-based stress reduction (MBSR) and mindfulness-based cognitive therapy (MBCT) are structured programs that integrate mindfulness practices into therapeutic contexts.

Benefits of Mindfulness Meditation:

- Stress Reduction: Mindfulness meditation has shown to be effective in reducing stress by promoting relaxation and modulating the body's stress response.

- Enhanced Focus and Concentration: Regular practice improves attention and concentration, cultivating a heightened state of awareness in daily activities.

- Emotional Regulation: Mindfulness equips individuals with tools to navigate and regulate emotions, fostering emotional resilience.

- Improved Well-Being: Studies suggest that mindfulness meditation contributes to overall well-being, enhancing life satisfaction and a positive outlook.

- Mind-Body Connection: The practice deepens the connection between the mind and body, promoting holistic health and self-care.

Conclusion:

Mindfulness meditation transcends being a mere technique; it is a transformative journey into the essence of being. As individuals engage in the intentional cultivation of present-moment awareness, they embark on a profound exploration of the mind, fostering a deep connection with the richness of each moment. Mindfulness meditation stands as an invitation to embrace the fullness of life, one breath at a time—a timeless practice that continues to unfold its wisdom in the tapestry of human experience.

Introduction to Mindfulness: Nurturing Presence in the Present Moment

In the midst of our fast-paced lives, characterized by constant movement and ever-present distractions, the concept of mindfulness has emerged as a beacon of serenity—a practice that invites individuals to pause, breathe, and cultivate a profound connection with the present moment. Rooted in ancient contemplative traditions and now embraced across diverse cultures, mindfulness offers a transformative journey into the heart of awareness, fostering a deep sense of presence and clarity.

Defining Mindfulness:

At its essence, mindfulness is the art of being fully engaged with the present moment, free from the entanglements of the past or the anxieties of the future. It involves bringing deliberate attention to one's thoughts, feelings, bodily sensations, and the surrounding environment with an attitude of openness and acceptance. Mindfulness is not about erasing thoughts or emotions but about observing them without judgment, allowing them to come and go like passing clouds in the sky.

The Breath as an Anchor:

A central aspect of mindfulness is the conscious awareness of the breath. The breath serves as an anchor, grounding individuals in the here and now. By focusing on the rhythmic inhalation and exhalation, practitioners cultivate a sense of presence, using the breath as a guide to tether the mind to the current moment. In the simplicity of each breath lies a doorway to tranquility and self-discovery.

Non-Judgmental Observation:

Mindfulness encourages a non-judgmental and compassionate observation of one's inner landscape. Rather than labeling thoughts or emotions as right or wrong, good or bad, individuals practice acknowledging them with acceptance. This non-reactive stance fosters a space for self-understanding, allowing individuals to navigate their experiences with a sense of equanimity.

Mindfulness Beyond Meditation:

While mindfulness is often associated with formal meditation practices, its application extends far beyond the meditation cushion. Everyday activities become opportunities for mindfulness—from savoring the flavors of a meal to walking with intentional awareness. The goal is to infuse mindfulness into the tapestry of daily life, transforming routine moments into opportunities for connection and presence.

Scientific Validation:

The benefits of mindfulness extend beyond subjective experiences, finding validation in scientific research. Studies have shown that regular mindfulness practice can lead to structural changes in the brain associated with improved attention, emotional regulation, and stress reduction. Mindfulness-based interventions have been incorporated into therapeutic approaches, demonstrating efficacy in addressing conditions such as anxiety, depression, and chronic pain.

Cultivating a Mindful Lifestyle:

Mindfulness is not a destination but a journey—an ongoing practice that unfolds gradually. It invites individuals to cultivate a mindful lifestyle, integrating present-moment awareness into various facets of life. As mindfulness becomes a way of being, individuals experience a heightened sense of clarity, resilience, and an enriched relationship with themselves and the world around them.

Conclusion:

In a world that often pulls us in myriad directions, mindfulness stands as a gentle reminder to return to the simplicity of the present moment. It is an invitation to savor the richness of life, unburdened by the past or the future. As we embark on this journey of mindfulness, we open ourselves to the transformative power of presence—one breath, one moment, and one step at a time. Mindfulness becomes a timeless practice, offering solace, insight, and a sanctuary within the ever-unfolding tapestry of our lives.

Building a Mindfulness Meditation Practice: Cultivating Inner Stillness and Presence

Embarking on the journey of building a mindfulness meditation practice is an empowering commitment to one's well-being and inner peace. In a world filled with constant stimuli and distractions, mindfulness meditation offers a sanctuary—a deliberate space to anchor oneself in the present moment, fostering clarity, calmness, and a deeper understanding of the mind. Here are essential steps to guide individuals in establishing and nurturing a meaningful mindfulness meditation practice.

1. Set Clear Intentions:

Begin by clarifying your intentions for embarking on a mindfulness journey. Whether it's stress reduction, enhanced focus, or overall well-being, a clear understanding of your goals provides a compass for your practice. Setting intentions creates a sense of purpose, aligning your efforts with the transformative potential of mindfulness.

2. Start with Short Sessions:

Establishing a meditation routine doesn't require extended periods of time. Begin with short sessions, perhaps five to ten minutes, and gradually extend as your comfort and familiarity with the practice grow. Consistency is key; even brief, daily sessions can yield profound benefits over time.

3. Create a Dedicated Space:

Designate a quiet and comfortable space for your mindfulness practice. It doesn't need to be elaborate; a corner of a room or a comfortable chair can suffice. The goal is to have a space that signals to your mind that this is a dedicated time for presence and self-reflection.

4. Focus on the Breath:

The breath is a fundamental anchor in mindfulness meditation. Pay attention to the natural rhythm of your breath, observing the inhalation and exhalation. When the mind wanders, gently bring it back to the breath. The breath serves as a constant and accessible point of focus in the ever-changing landscape of thoughts.

5. Embrace Non-Judgmental Awareness:

Cultivate an attitude of non-judgmental awareness toward your thoughts and feelings. Instead of labeling them as good or bad, simply observe them with curiosity and acceptance. This approach fosters a compassionate relationship with your own inner experiences.

6. Utilize Guided Meditations:

Guided meditations, led by experienced instructors, can provide structure and support, especially for beginners. Many resources, including apps and online platforms, offer a variety of guided mindfulness sessions tailored to different goals and timeframes.

7. Be Patient and Gentle with Yourself:

Mindfulness meditation is a skill that develops over time. Be patient and gentle with yourself, understanding that moments of distraction are natural. The essence lies in the return to awareness. Approach your practice with self-compassion, recognizing that it is okay to have varying experiences during meditation.

8. Integrate Mindfulness into Daily Life:

Extend the benefits of mindfulness beyond formal meditation sessions by incorporating it into daily activities. Practice mindful eating, walking, or even moments of intentional breathing throughout the day. This integration reinforces mindfulness as a way of life rather than a confined practice.

9. Explore Different Approaches:

Mindfulness is diverse, and various approaches suit different individuals. Explore different meditation techniques—body scan, loving-kindness meditation, or mindfulness of emotions—to find what resonates with you. Diversity in practice can keep your meditation journey dynamic and engaging.

10. Celebrate Progress:

Celebrate the progress you make in your mindfulness meditation practice. Recognize the moments of increased presence, reduced reactivity, or enhanced self-awareness. Mindfulness is a continuous journey, and acknowledging your growth fosters motivation and a positive relationship with the practice.

Building a mindfulness meditation practice is a personal and evolving endeavor. With commitment, patience, and an open heart, individuals can cultivate a practice that not only enhances their mental well-being but also deepens their connection with the richness of each present moment.

Visualization and Imagery

Harnessing the Power of the Mind's Eye

Visualization and imagery are potent cognitive tools that tap into the remarkable capacity of the mind to create and simulate experiences. By harnessing the power of mental imagery, individuals can enhance performance, reduce stress, and cultivate a positive mindset. Whether applied in sports, therapy, or personal development, visualization and imagery serve as bridges between thought and manifestation, unlocking the potential within the realms of imagination.

Understanding Visualization:

Visualization involves creating vivid mental images or scenes in the mind's eye. It's the process of mentally rehearsing or picturing an activity or outcome. This technique is often used in various contexts, such as sports training, public speaking, or achieving personal goals. Visualization engages multiple senses, allowing individuals to immerse themselves in a mental representation of the desired scenario.

Key Elements of Visualization:

- Clarity: The more vivid and detailed the mental images, the more effective the visualization. Clarity involves not only seeing images but also engaging other senses—feeling, hearing, and even smelling or tasting, depending on the imagined scenario.

- Emotion: Infusing visualization with positive emotions amplifies its impact. By connecting emotionally to the imagined experience, individuals can enhance motivation and cultivate a positive mindset.

- Repetition: Like physical practice, mental rehearsal benefits from repetition. Regular visualization sessions reinforce neural pathways, making the imagined experience more familiar and attainable.

Applications of Visualization:

Sports Performance:

Athletes often use visualization to mentally rehearse their performances. By visualizing successful outcomes, they enhance muscle memory, build confidence, and reduce anxiety. This mental preparation can lead to improved actual performance on the field or in competition.

Stress Reduction:

Visualization is a powerful tool for managing stress and anxiety. Individuals can create mental images of serene and calming scenes, engaging in a virtual retreat that promotes relaxation and a sense of inner peace.

Goal Achievement:

Visualization is a valuable tool for goal setting and achievement. By picturing oneself reaching specific milestones, individuals create a roadmap for success. This mental blueprint can enhance focus, motivation, and perseverance.

Creative Endeavors:

Artists, writers, and creatives often use visualization to ideate and plan their projects. Envisioning the details of a painting, the plot of a story, or the design of a product helps in the creative process.

Understanding Imagery:

Imagery encompasses a broader spectrum of mental representations that go beyond the visual domain. It includes sensations, emotions, and perceptions conjured in the mind. While visualization is a specific form of imagery focusing on the visual aspect, imagery, in general, can involve any sensory or experiential component.

Key Elements of Imagery:

Multi-Sensory Engagement: Imagery can involve not only visual elements but also auditory, tactile, olfactory, and gustatory components. Engaging multiple senses enriches the mental experience.

Associative and Dissociative Imagery: Associative imagery involves seeing and experiencing an event through one's own eyes, while dissociative imagery involves viewing oneself from an external perspective. Both perspectives offer unique insights and applications.

Applications of Imagery:

Pain Management:

Imagery is used in pain management techniques, where individuals mentally create scenes or sensations that counteract or distract from physical discomfort.

Therapeutic Intervention:

Therapists use imagery to help individuals explore and reframe experiences. Guided imagery can assist in processing emotions, confronting fears, and promoting relaxation.

Memory Enhancement:

Imagery is a mnemonic device that aids memory. Creating vivid mental images associated with information enhances retention and recall.

Mind-Body Connection:

Imagery is integral to practices like guided meditation and mindfulness. By immersing oneself in positive mental images, individuals can promote overall well-being and stress reduction.

Conclusion:

Visualization and imagery exemplify the remarkable capabilities of the human mind to transcend reality and influence experiences. Whether employed for achieving goals, managing stress, or fostering creativity, these cognitive tools offer a gateway to the transformative potential of the mind's eye. Through intentional and focused practice, individuals can unlock the creative, motivational, and healing capacities inherent in the vivid landscapes of their imagination.

Harnessing the Imagination for Relaxation: A Journey into Tranquil Inner Landscapes

In the bustling pace of modern life, where stress often feels like an unwelcome companion, the imagination becomes a sanctuary—a haven that holds the key to relaxation and tranquility. By intentionally directing the mind's creative power, individuals can embark on a journey into serene inner landscapes, fostering a sense of calmness and rejuvenation. Here, we explore the art of harnessing the imagination for relaxation—a practice that transcends the ordinary to embrace the extraordinary realms within.

Creating Mental Retreats:

Imagination serves as a passport to mental retreats where stress dissipates, and calmness prevails. Close your eyes and envision a tranquil setting—a secluded beach, a lush forest, or a mountain retreat. Engage all your senses in this mental imagery. Feel the warmth of the sun, hear the rustle of leaves, smell the crisp mountain air. As you immerse yourself in this created sanctuary, your mind responds by inducing a state of relaxation.

Guided Imagery for Stress Reduction:

Guided imagery is a powerful tool for stress reduction. With the guidance of a narrator or through self-directed scripts, individuals can imagine soothing scenes that transport them away from stressors. This might involve picturing a peaceful garden, visualizing stress as a balloon floating away, or imagining tension melting like ice under a warm sun. Guided imagery taps into the mind's capacity to influence the body's stress response, promoting a sense of calm and balance.

Immersing in Sensory Richness:

The imagination is not limited to visuals alone; it extends to a rich tapestry of sensations. Create mental scenarios that engage all your senses. Picture yourself in a cozy cabin by a crackling fireplace, feel the warmth of the fire, hear the wood popping, and even imagine the aroma of the burning wood. By immersing yourself in this sensory richness, you activate a holistic response that transcends mere visualization, inviting a deeper state of relaxation.

Transformation through Positive Visualization:

Positive visualization involves using the imagination to envision desired outcomes and experiences. Instead of dwelling on stressors, visualize positive scenarios that evoke joy, accomplishment, and contentment. Whether it's acing a presentation, achieving a personal goal, or basking in a moment of triumph, the mind's ability to pre-experience success contributes to a positive mindset and reduced stress.

Mindful Imagination in Meditation:

In meditation, the imagination becomes a gateway to profound states of relaxation. Mindful imagination involves cultivating a receptive awareness of mental images without attachment. Picture a gentle stream, let it flow, and observe the images that arise without judgment. By allowing the imagination to unfold organically, meditation becomes a dynamic exploration of the mind's capacity for tranquility.

The Power of Breath and Visualization:

Combine the calming influence of breath with the vividness of visualization. As you inhale, imagine drawing in relaxation and peace. With each exhale, visualize releasing tension and stress. This synchronized dance of breath and imagination enhances the mind-body connection, creating a harmonious rhythm that promotes relaxation.

Conclusion:

In the realm of relaxation, the imagination emerges as a potent ally—a source of solace, inspiration, and rejuvenation. By consciously harnessing the power of the mind's eye, individuals can embark on journeys into tranquil landscapes, free from the grip of stress. Through guided imagery, positive visualization, and mindful exploration, the imagination becomes a conduit to inner peace—a timeless practice that invites individuals to rediscover the art of relaxation within the boundless realms of their own creativity.

Creating Mental Retreats: A Gateway to Inner Serenity

In the midst of life's whirlwind, finding moments of respite becomes essential for maintaining mental well-being. Creating mental retreats offers a transformative practice, allowing individuals to step into the sanctuary of their own minds, away from the demands and stressors of the external world. This intentional journey into tranquility becomes a powerful tool for relaxation, rejuvenation, and the cultivation of inner serenity.

Choosing Your Retreat Space:

Begin by selecting a mental space that resonates with a sense of calmness and peace. It might be a pristine beach, a secluded mountain cabin, a tranquil garden, or any setting that holds personal significance. The key is to envision a space where you feel safe, relaxed, and free from external pressures.

Engaging the Senses:

Immerse yourself in the sensory richness of your mental retreat. Close your eyes and vividly picture the details. Feel the warmth of the sun on your skin, hear the gentle rustle of leaves, and smell the subtle fragrance of flowers. Engaging multiple senses enhances the depth of the experience, making the mental retreat more immersive and effective.

Guided Imagery for Enhanced Relaxation:

Guided imagery scripts or recordings can be invaluable in enhancing the effectiveness of mental retreats. These scripts provide gentle guidance, prompting you to visualize specific details or scenarios. Whether it's a calming beach walk, a peaceful forest hike, or a soothing journey through a meadow, guided imagery amplifies the relaxation response, making the mental retreat more structured and enjoyable.

Breathing as an Anchor:

Incorporate mindful breathing as an anchor during your mental retreats. Pay attention to the rhythm of your breath, allowing it to synchronize with the imagined environment. Inhale deeply, drawing in the tranquility of your mental retreat, and exhale slowly, releasing any tension or stress. The breath becomes a bridge between the physical and the imagined, deepening the sense of relaxation.

Timelessness and Personalization:

Mental retreats are not bound by time constraints. They can be as brief or extended as needed. Whether you have a few minutes during a hectic day or can dedicate a more extended period, the beauty of mental retreats lies in their adaptability to your schedule. Additionally, feel free to personalize your mental retreat—add details that bring you joy, create scenarios that resonate with your preferences, and make it uniquely yours.

Mindful Presence in Your Retreat:

Practice mindful presence during your mental retreats. As you visualize your serene environment, let go of distractions and immerse yourself fully in the present moment. Be aware of the sensations, emotions, and thoughts that arise. Mindful presence enhances the depth of the experience, fostering a profound connection with your inner world.

Transitioning Back to the Present:

When you're ready to conclude your mental retreat, do so gradually. Bring your awareness back to your physical surroundings. Take a few grounding breaths and carry the sense of tranquility with you into your daily activities. The ability to transition seamlessly between your mental retreat and the external world is a valuable skill, ensuring that the benefits of relaxation extend beyond the confines of the imagination.

Conclusion:

Creating mental retreats is a practice that invites individuals to reclaim a sense of control over their mental landscapes. In the quiet recesses of the mind, where the external noise diminishes, lies the potential for profound relaxation and rejuvenation. By crafting and revisiting these inner sanctuaries, individuals cultivate a timeless resource for navigating life's challenges with a renewed sense of calm and resilience.

Progressive Muscle Relaxation

A Guided Journey to Physical and Mental Harmony

In the pursuit of well-being, an array of relaxation techniques has emerged, each offering a unique pathway to tranquility. Among these, Progressive Muscle Relaxation (PMR) stands out as a systematic and effective method for reducing muscle tension, alleviating stress, and promoting a profound sense of relaxation. This evidence-based technique, pioneered by Dr. Edmund Jacobson in the early 20th century, has since become a widely utilized tool in the realm of stress management and holistic health.

Understanding Progressive Muscle Relaxation (PMR):

At its core, PMR is a mind-body technique that involves the intentional tensing and subsequent relaxation of specific muscle groups throughout the body. The fundamental principle behind PMR is based on the reciprocal relationship between muscle tension and relaxation. By deliberately tensing muscles and then releasing that tension, individuals enhance their awareness of the sensations associated with muscle relaxation. This heightened awareness contributes to a reduction in overall muscle tension and, subsequently, a release of stress.

The Progressive Muscle Relaxation Process:

Preparation:

Begin by finding a quiet and comfortable space where you won't be interrupted. Sit or lie down in a relaxed position, ensuring that your clothing is loose and comfortable. Take a few deep breaths to initiate a sense of calmness.

Muscle Tensing:

The PMR process involves systematically tensing and then relaxing different muscle groups. Start with a specific muscle group, such as the muscles in your hands or forehead. Tense these muscles for about 5-10 seconds, focusing on the sensation of tension. Make sure to isolate the chosen muscle group without straining or causing discomfort.

Release and Relaxation:

After tensing, release the tension abruptly, allowing the muscles to relax completely. As you release the tension, pay close attention to the contrasting sensations of relaxation. Feel the warmth, heaviness, and the absence of tension in the relaxed muscles.

Progress Through Muscle Groups:

Progress through different muscle groups, moving systematically from one area of the body to another. Common sequences include starting with the hands, moving to the arms, shoulders, face, neck, chest, abdomen, back, hips, and legs. The goal is to cover the entire body, paying attention to each muscle group.

Breathing and Mindfulness:

Throughout the PMR process, focus on your breath. Breathe naturally and calmly, allowing your breath to complement the rhythm of muscle tension and relaxation. Engage in mindfulness, directing your attention to the present moment and the sensations within your body.

Complete Relaxation:

Conclude the PMR session with a few moments of complete relaxation. Allow your entire body to remain in a state of ease, appreciating the profound relaxation you have cultivated.

Benefits of Progressive Muscle Relaxation:

Stress Reduction:

PMR is renowned for its ability to reduce overall stress levels. The deliberate release of muscle tension sends signals to the nervous system to activate the relaxation response, counteracting the physiological effects of stress.

Muscle Tension Relief:

Individuals who experience chronic muscle tension, whether due to stress or physical conditions, often find relief through regular practice of PMR. The technique promotes a heightened awareness of muscle tension, enabling individuals to release it consciously.

Improved Sleep:

PMR is a valuable tool for improving sleep quality. By engaging in PMR before bedtime, individuals can create a state of physical and mental relaxation conducive to a restful night's sleep.

Anxiety Management:

As a relaxation technique, PMR is effective in managing anxiety. By breaking the cycle of muscle tension associated with anxiety, individuals can experience a sense of calmness and control.

Enhanced Mind-Body Connection:

Through the systematic focus on different muscle groups, PMR enhances the mind-body connection. Individuals become more attuned to the physical sensations within their bodies, fostering a deeper understanding of the interplay between mental and physical well-being.

Incorporating Progressive Muscle Relaxation into Daily Life:

Regular Practice:

To experience the full benefits of PMR, consistency is key. Aim to practice PMR regularly, ideally once or twice a day. Short sessions, lasting 10-20 minutes, can be highly effective.

Adaptability:

PMR is versatile and can be adapted to various settings. Whether at home, in the workplace, or during moments of heightened stress, individuals can engage in PMR to promote relaxation and restore balance.

Integration with Other Relaxation Techniques:

Combine PMR with other relaxation techniques, such as deep breathing, guided imagery, or mindfulness meditation. The synergistic effect of these practices can amplify the overall relaxation response.

Incorporate into Bedtime Routine:

Consider incorporating PMR into your bedtime routine. As part of your pre-sleep ritual, engaging in PMR can signal to your body and mind that it's time to unwind and prepare for rest.

Conclusion:

Progressive Muscle Relaxation offers a tangible and accessible approach to relaxation, empowering individuals to actively participate in their well-being. Through the deliberate release of muscle tension, individuals not only experience physical relaxation but also cultivate a heightened awareness of the mind-body connection. As a versatile and evidence-based technique, PMR stands as a valuable tool in the toolkit of stress management, promoting a state of harmony between body and mind in the journey toward optimal well-being.

Techniques for Physical Tension Release

Releasing physical tension is crucial for maintaining overall well-being, as persistent tension can contribute to stress, discomfort, and even impact mental health. Various techniques can help release physical tension, promoting relaxation and a sense of balance. Here are several effective methods:

Progressive Muscle Relaxation (PMR):

As mentioned earlier, PMR involves systematically tensing and then relaxing different muscle groups in the body. This technique helps release built-up tension and enhances the mind-body connection. By focusing on each muscle group, individuals become more aware of tension patterns and learn to release them intentionally.

Deep Breathing Exercises:

Deep breathing techniques, such as diaphragmatic breathing or belly breathing, encourage the use of the diaphragm for inhalation. This type of breathing helps activate the body's relaxation response, reducing muscle tension and promoting a sense of calm. Deep breaths also increase oxygen flow to the muscles, aiding in their relaxation.

Stretching and Yoga:

Engaging in stretching exercises and yoga is an effective way to release physical tension. These practices not only enhance flexibility but also encourage mindfulness and body awareness. Stretching helps elongate muscles, alleviating tightness and reducing overall tension.

Self-Massage:

Self-massage techniques, such as using foam rollers, massage balls, or simply using your hands, can target specific areas of tension. Focus on areas like the neck, shoulders, back, and legs. Applying gentle pressure and circular motions can help release tight muscles and improve blood circulation.

Warm Baths or Showers:

Immersing yourself in a warm bath or taking a hot shower can promote relaxation and help release physical tension. The warm water soothes muscles, increases blood flow, and provides a calming effect on the nervous system.

Guided Imagery and Visualization:

Visualization techniques involve imagining peaceful and calming scenes, allowing the mind to influence the body's physical state. Visualization can be combined with deep breathing to enhance relaxation. Envisioning tension melting away or picturing a serene environment can contribute to the release of physical tension.

Tai Chi:

Tai Chi is a mind-body practice that combines slow, deliberate movements with deep breathing and meditation. This ancient Chinese martial art promotes flexibility, balance, and relaxation. The flowing movements of Tai Chi can help release tension and improve overall physical well-being.

Biofeedback:

Biofeedback is a technique that uses electronic monitoring to provide information about physiological processes such as muscle tension, heart rate, and skin temperature. Through visual or auditory feedback, individuals can learn to consciously control and release tension in real-time.

Guided Progressive Relaxation Audios:

Utilizing guided audio recordings or apps that lead you through progressive relaxation exercises can be beneficial. These resources often provide instructions for tensing and relaxing specific muscle groups, making it easier for individuals to follow along and release tension.

Mindfulness Meditation:

Mindfulness meditation involves cultivating a non-judgmental awareness of the present moment. By paying attention to the sensations in the body, individuals can become more aware of areas of tension. Mindfulness meditation encourages letting go of tension and promotes a sense of ease.

Heat and Cold Therapy:

Applying heat or cold to tense areas can help soothe muscles and reduce tension. Warm compresses or heating pads can relax tight muscles, while cold packs can help reduce inflammation and numb pain in specific areas.

Aromatherapy:

The use of calming scents, such as lavender or chamomile, through aromatherapy can contribute to physical relaxation. Essential oils can be applied topically or diffused in the air to create a soothing environment.

It's important to note that everyone is different, and what works for one person may vary for another. Experimenting with different techniques and finding what resonates best for you can contribute to an effective strategy for releasing physical tension and promoting a sense of relaxation and well-being.

Integrating Relaxation into Daily Routines

Integrating relaxation into daily routines is essential for maintaining overall well-being and managing stress. By incorporating relaxation techniques into your daily schedule, you create moments of calmness and self-care. Here are various methods and examples for seamlessly integrating relaxation into your daily routines:

Morning Routine:

- Mindful Wake-Up: Instead of rushing out of bed, take a few minutes to wake up mindfully. Practice deep breathing or gentle stretching to start your day with a sense of calm.

- Positive Affirmations: Incorporate positive affirmations into your morning routine. Repeat affirmations that promote relaxation and set a positive tone for the day.

Commute:

- Mindful Breathing: Practice mindful breathing during your commute. Use the time to focus on your breath, inhaling and exhaling slowly to create a sense of relaxation.

- Podcasts or Relaxing Music: Listen to podcasts or calming music during your commute to create a soothing atmosphere.

Work Breaks:

- Stretching Exercises: Take short breaks throughout the workday to stretch your body. Simple stretching exercises can alleviate tension and improve focus.

- Deep Breathing at Your Desk: Incorporate deep breathing exercises at your desk to manage stress. Inhale deeply, hold for a few seconds, and exhale slowly.

Lunchtime:

- Mindful Eating: Practice mindful eating during lunch. Focus on the taste, texture, and aroma of your food, allowing yourself to fully enjoy the meal and take a mental break.

- Short Walk: Take a short walk after lunch to get fresh air and clear your mind.

Afternoon Slump:

- Quick Meditation: Allocate a few minutes for a quick meditation session in the afternoon. Find a quiet space, close your eyes, and focus on your breath to recharge.

- Desk Yoga: Incorporate simple yoga stretches at your desk to release tension and boost energy.

Evening Routine:

- Digital Detox: Establish a digital detox routine in the evening. Turn off electronic devices at least an hour before bedtime to promote relaxation.

- Reading or Journaling: Wind down with a good book or engage in journaling to reflect on your day. These activities can be calming and help transition to a restful night.

Before Bed:

- Progressive Muscle Relaxation (PMR): Practice PMR before bedtime to release physical tension. Tense and relax different muscle groups to induce a state of relaxation.

- Guided Sleep Meditation: Listen to a guided sleep meditation to ease your mind and prepare for a restful night.

Family Time:

- Mindful Family Activities: Engage in mindful family activities, such as a nature walk or a board game night. These activities promote relaxation and strengthen family bonds.

- Shared Relaxation: Encourage your family members to join you in relaxation practices, such as deep breathing or meditation.

Weekend Rituals:

- Nature Outings: Spend time in nature during the weekends. Whether it's a hike, a picnic, or a visit to a park, being in natural surroundings can be incredibly relaxing.

- Self-Care Day: Dedicate a day to self-care activities, such as a spa day at home, reading, or enjoying hobbies that bring joy and relaxation.

Mealtime:

- Mindful Eating Practices: Extend the practice of mindful eating to dinner. Focus on the flavors and textures of your food, fostering a relaxed dining experience.

- Family Dinners: If possible, incorporate family dinners into your routine. Shared meals provide an opportunity for relaxation and connection.

Bedtime Routine:

- Relaxing Bath: Incorporate a relaxing bath into your bedtime routine. Add calming essential oils or bath salts to enhance the soothing experience.

- Gratitude Practice: End your day with a gratitude practice. Reflect on positive aspects of your day to promote a sense of contentment and relaxation.

Remember, the key is to find what works best for you and tailor these examples to fit your lifestyle. Consistently integrating relaxation into your daily routines contributes to a more balanced and stress-resistant life.

Yoga for Stress Relief

Nurturing Harmony in Body and Mind

In the fast-paced and demanding landscape of modern life, stress has become an almost inevitable companion. However, amidst the hustle and bustle, yoga emerges as a powerful ally in cultivating serenity and balance. More than a physical exercise, yoga is a holistic practice that intertwines breath, movement, and mindfulness, offering a profound pathway to stress relief and overall well-being.

The Essence of Yoga:

At its core, yoga is a centuries-old practice that originated in ancient India. It encompasses a diverse range of techniques designed to unite the mind, body, and spirit. The word "yoga" itself derives from the Sanskrit root "yuj," meaning to yoke or unite. Through a combination of physical postures (asanas), breath control (pranayama), meditation, and ethical principles, yoga seeks to create harmony within and foster a connection with the present moment.

Yoga Asanas for Stress Relief:

Child's Pose (Balasana):

- Kneel on the mat, sit back on your heels, and extend your arms forward with your forehead resting on the ground.

- This gentle stretch relaxes the spine and promotes a sense of surrender, releasing tension in the back and shoulders.

Corpse Pose (Savasana):

- Lie on your back with arms by your sides, palms facing up, and legs extended.

- Savasana is a relaxation pose that allows for deep rest and rejuvenation, calming the nervous system and reducing overall tension.

Downward-Facing Dog (Adho Mukha Svanasana):

- Begin on your hands and knees, lift your hips toward the ceiling, and straighten your legs.
- Downward Dog elongates the spine, stretches the hamstrings, and invigorates the entire body, promoting a sense of openness and release.

Cat-Cow Pose (Marjaryasana-Bitilasana):

- Move between arching your back (Cow Pose) and rounding it (Cat Pose) in a flowing motion.
- This dynamic sequence increases spinal flexibility and helps release tension in the back and neck.

Seated Forward Bend (Paschimottanasana):

- Sit with legs extended, hinge at the hips, and reach toward your toes.
- Paschimottanasana is a calming forward bend that stretches the spine, hamstrings, and lower back, promoting relaxation.

Tree Pose (Vrikshasana):

- Stand on one leg, bring the sole of the opposite foot to the inner thigh or calf, and balance.
- Tree Pose cultivates balance and focus, grounding the practitioner and calming the mind.

Pranayama for Stress Reduction:

Deep Belly Breathing (Diaphragmatic Breathing):

- Inhale deeply through the nose, allowing the belly to expand, and exhale slowly through the mouth.
- Diaphragmatic breathing activates the body's relaxation response, calming the nervous system and reducing stress.

Alternate Nostril Breathing (Nadi Shodhana):

- Close one nostril with the thumb, inhale through the other nostril, then close the opposite nostril and exhale.

- Nadi Shodhana balances the left and right sides of the brain, promoting mental clarity and reducing anxiety.

Ujjayi Breath (Ocean Breath):

- Inhale deeply through the nose, constrict the back of the throat, and exhale with a soft "ha" sound.

- Ujjayi breath enhances focus, warms the body, and encourages a meditative state.

Mindfulness and Meditation in Yoga:

Mindful Awareness:

- During yoga practice, cultivate mindful awareness by paying attention to each movement, breath, and sensation.

- Mindfulness in yoga fosters a present-moment focus, helping alleviate stress by redirecting the mind from future worries or past concerns.

Guided Meditation:

- Integrate guided meditation into your yoga routine, either during asana practice or as a separate session.

- Guided meditation provides a mental retreat, offering relaxation and stress relief through visualization and focused awareness.

Holistic Well-Being through Yoga:

Stress Reduction at the Neurological Level:

- Regular yoga practice has been shown to modulate the body's stress response by influencing the autonomic nervous system.

- The combination of asanas, pranayama, and meditation helps regulate the sympathetic and parasympathetic nervous systems, promoting a balanced state.

Improved Emotional Regulation:

- Yoga encourages emotional awareness and regulation by fostering a mind-body connection.

- Mindfulness in yoga allows individuals to observe and manage emotions, reducing reactivity to stressors and promoting emotional resilience.

Enhanced Physical Well-Being:

- Beyond stress relief, yoga enhances physical health by improving flexibility, strength, and overall cardiovascular fitness.

- The physical benefits of yoga contribute to a sense of well-being, reducing physical discomfort and tension associated with stress.

Community and Support:

- Joining a yoga class or community provides a supportive environment, fostering a sense of connection and social well-being.

- The communal aspect of yoga can alleviate feelings of isolation and enhance overall mental health.

In Conclusion:

Yoga is a holistic and accessible approach to stress relief, offering a sanctuary for individuals seeking balance amid life's demands. Through the integration of physical postures, breath awareness, and mindfulness, yoga becomes a transformative practice that extends beyond the mat, nurturing harmony in both body and mind. Whether you're a seasoned yogi or a beginner, the essence of yoga lies in its adaptability and inclusivity, making it a versatile tool for stress reduction and overall well-being.

Gentle Yoga Poses for Relaxation: Nurturing the Body and Calming the Mind

In the realm of yoga, there exists a gentle and soothing practice tailored to provide relaxation and restore a sense of calmness. Gentle yoga, with its slow and mindful approach, offers a sanctuary for individuals seeking to unwind, release tension, and invite a deep sense of relaxation into their lives. Here are several gentle yoga poses that foster relaxation, promoting a harmonious connection between the body and the mind.

Child's Pose (Balasana):

- Kneel on the mat, sit back on your heels, and extend your arms forward with your forehead resting on the ground.

- Child's Pose gently stretches the back, hips, and thighs, promoting a sense of surrender and release in the spine.

Cat-Cow Pose (Marjaryasana-Bitilasana):

- Begin on your hands and knees, alternately arch your back (Cow Pose) and round it (Cat Pose).

- This flowing sequence enhances spinal flexibility, massages the spine, and helps release tension in the back and neck.

Legs Up the Wall (Viparita Karani):

- Sit close to a wall, lie on your back, and extend your legs up the wall.

- Viparita Karani is a restorative inversion that promotes relaxation by draining tension from the legs and encouraging blood flow back to the heart.

Supported Bridge Pose (Setu Bandhasana):

- Lie on your back, bend your knees, and lift your hips. Place a prop such as a block or bolster under your sacrum.

- Supported Bridge Pose gently stretches the spine and opens the chest, offering a restorative backbend for relaxation.

Seated Forward Bend (Paschimottanasana):

- Sit with legs extended, hinge at the hips, and reach toward your toes.

- Paschimottanasana stretches the spine, hamstrings, and lower back, promoting a calming effect on the nervous system.

Corpse Pose (Savasana):

- Lie on your back with arms by your sides, palms facing up, and legs extended.

- Savasana is a classic relaxation pose that allows for complete surrender, calming the mind and releasing tension throughout the body.

Butterfly Pose (Baddha Konasana):

- Sit with the soles of your feet together and knees bent outward. Hold your feet and gently press your knees toward the floor.

- Butterfly Pose opens the hips and groin, relieving tension and promoting a sense of ease.

Supported Child's Pose (Salamba Balasana):

- Place a bolster or pillow lengthwise on the mat. Kneel with your knees on either side of the bolster, then lower your torso onto the support.

- Supported Child's Pose provides extra comfort and relaxation, particularly for the lower back and hips.

Thread the Needle Pose (Parsva Balasana):

- Begin on your hands and knees. Slide your right arm under your left arm, lowering your shoulder and ear to the mat.

- Thread the Needle Pose releases tension in the shoulders and upper back, offering a gentle twist for relaxation.

Easy Pose with Forward Fold (Sukhasana with Forward Fold):

- Sit cross-legged and hinge at the hips, folding forward with your arms extended.

- This variation of Easy Pose gently stretches the back and promotes relaxation in the hips.

Extended Triangle Pose (Utthita Trikonasana):

- Stand with your feet wide apart, extend your arms, and reach forward over your front leg.

- Extended Triangle Pose provides a gentle stretch for the sides of the body, hips, and hamstrings, fostering relaxation.

Supported Reclining Bound Angle Pose (Supta Baddha Konasana):

- Lie on your back, bend your knees, and bring the soles of your feet together. Support your knees with props.

- Supported Reclining Bound Angle Pose opens the chest and hips while providing support for total relaxation.

Mindful Breath with Poses:

- Inhale deeply through the nose, and exhale slowly through the mouth.

- Incorporate mindful breathing with each pose, emphasizing the connection between breath and movement for enhanced relaxation.

Guidelines for Gentle Yoga:

- Listen to your body and avoid pushing into discomfort.

- Use props, such as bolsters, blankets, or blocks, to support your practice.

- Focus on slow, intentional movements and breath awareness.

In Conclusion:

Gentle yoga invites individuals to embark on a journey of self-care, embracing the nurturing power of mindful movement and breath. Through these poses, practitioners can create a sanctuary for relaxation, fostering a deep sense of calmness and balance. Whether you are new to yoga or seeking a gentle practice, these poses provide an accessible and soothing way to unwind, release tension, and cultivate relaxation in both the body and the mind.

Incorporating Yoga into a Busy Lifestyle: A Balancing Act for Well-Being

In the midst of hectic schedules and demanding routines, finding moments of tranquility and self-care is essential for maintaining overall well-being. Yoga, with its holistic approach to physical and mental health, can be a beacon of balance amid the chaos of a busy lifestyle. Here are practical strategies for seamlessly integrating yoga into your daily routine, fostering a sense of calmness and mindfulness even amidst a bustling schedule.

1. Start with Short Sessions:

- Recognize that yoga doesn't require lengthy sessions. Begin with short, focused practices that can easily fit into your schedule.

- A 10 to 15-minute yoga routine in the morning or before bedtime can make a significant impact on your overall well-being.

2. Create a Dedicated Space:

- Designate a small area in your home or office for yoga practice. This can be a corner with a yoga mat, cushion, or a comfortable chair.

- Having a dedicated space helps signal to your mind that it's time to pause and engage in mindful movement.

3. Utilize Yoga Apps or Online Classes:

- Leverage technology to your advantage. Numerous yoga apps and online platforms offer a variety of classes tailored to different durations and skill levels.

- Choose sessions that align with your available time, whether it's a quick flow during a break or a longer practice on weekends.

4. Integrate Yoga into Daily Activities:

- Infuse yoga into your routine by incorporating mindful movements throughout the day.

- Practice deep breathing while commuting, stretch during short breaks, or incorporate gentle stretches before bedtime.

5. Prioritize Consistency Over Duration:

- Rather than aiming for lengthy sessions, focus on consistent practice. Even a few minutes of daily yoga can lead to noticeable improvements in flexibility, stress reduction, and overall well-being.

- Consistency is key, and establishing a daily habit is more sustainable than sporadic, longer sessions.

6. Embrace Mindful Breathing:

- Incorporate mindful breathing exercises into your day. Whether you're in a meeting, commuting, or waiting in line, take a moment to focus on your breath.

- Mindful breathing can be a discreet yet powerful way to introduce elements of yoga into your busy schedule, promoting relaxation and mental clarity.

7. Lunchtime or Office Yoga:

- Use your lunch break as an opportunity for a brief yoga session. Find a quiet spot, use a chair for support, and engage in seated stretches or simple standing poses.

- Office yoga can alleviate tension and rejuvenate your body and mind for the remainder of the day.

8. Establish Morning or Evening Rituals:

- Integrate yoga into your morning or evening rituals to create a sense of routine.

- A short yoga practice upon waking can energize your body, while an evening routine can signal the transition to relaxation and prepare you for a restful night.

9. Involve Family or Friends:

- Turn yoga into a shared activity by involving family members or friends. Consider practicing together, whether it's a gentle flow or partner yoga.

- Shared yoga sessions can create a supportive environment and reinforce the importance of self-care within your social circle.

10. Be Kind to Yourself:

- Release the notion of perfection. Understand that some days may be busier than others, and your yoga practice might be shorter or less structured.

- Be kind to yourself and celebrate the moments you dedicate to self-care, regardless of their duration.

11. Attend Short Classes or Workshops:

- Explore local yoga studios or community centers that offer shorter classes or workshops. Many places provide express sessions designed to fit into busy schedules.

- Attending occasional classes can offer guidance, variety, and a sense of community.

12. Combine Yoga with Other Activities:

- Integrate yoga with other daily activities. For instance, practice standing poses while waiting for your coffee to brew or incorporate gentle stretches while watching TV.

- Combining yoga with routine tasks seamlessly infuses mindfulness into your daily life.

In Conclusion:

Incorporating yoga into a busy lifestyle is not about adding another item to your to-do list; it's about weaving moments of self-care into the fabric of your day. By embracing the flexibility and adaptability of yoga, you can create a sustainable practice that supports your well-being amidst the demands of a busy life. Whether it's a few mindful breaths, a quick stretch, or a dedicated session, integrating yoga into your routine can be a transformative journey towards balance and harmony.

Art and Creativity

Unleashing the Power of Imagination

Art and creativity are the dynamic forces that breathe life into the human experience, transcending boundaries and connecting individuals across cultures and epochs. The canvas of creativity is vast and diverse, encompassing visual arts, literature, music, dance, theater, and more. In exploring the profound interplay between art and creativity, one discovers not only a means of expression but a transformative journey that fosters innovation, self-discovery, and a deeper understanding of the world.

The Essence of Creativity:

At its core, creativity is the ability to generate novel ideas, forge connections between seemingly unrelated concepts, and envision possibilities beyond the ordinary. It is an intrinsic aspect of human nature, driving innovation and progress in every sphere of life. Creativity manifests in myriad forms, from the strokes of a painter's brush to the symphony of a composer's notes, from the eloquence of a writer's prose to the ingenuity of a scientist's experiments.

Art as a Medium of Expression:

Art, as the offspring of creativity, serves as a powerful medium of expression. Through visual elements, emotions, and narratives, artists communicate complex ideas, cultural nuances, and individual perspectives. Artistic expression becomes a language that transcends linguistic barriers, offering a universal means of connection and understanding.

The Transformative Power of Art:

Art possesses a unique ability to transform both the creator and the audience. For the artist, the act of creation is a journey of self-discovery and introspection. It provides a space for exploring emotions, grappling with concepts, and giving form to the intangible. The artist engages in a dialogue with their inner self, bringing forth ideas and narratives that may have remained dormant.

For the audience, engaging with art is an immersive experience that elicits emotions, provokes thoughts, and sparks contemplation. A painting, a piece of music, or a theatrical performance has the potential to evoke joy, sadness, nostalgia, or introspection. Through this shared emotional resonance, art fosters empathy and connection, uniting individuals in a collective exploration of the human condition.

Creativity as a Catalyst for Innovation:

In the realms of science, technology, and business, creativity is the driving force behind innovation. The ability to think outside conventional boundaries, question existing paradigms, and envision new solutions is essential for progress. Creative thinking allows individuals to approach challenges with fresh perspectives, leading to breakthroughs, inventions, and advancements.

Innovation often emerges from the intersection of disciplines, where diverse ideas converge to create something entirely novel. This interdisciplinary approach mirrors the cross-pollination of ideas seen in the arts, where different forms of expression blend to produce innovative works that challenge conventions.

Artistic Exploration of Identity and Society:

Art has long been a mirror reflecting the complexities of identity and society. Through literature, visual arts, and performing arts, artists explore issues of race, gender, politics, and cultural identity. Artistic creations serve as a commentary on the human experience, provoking conversations about societal norms, injustices, and the quest for equality.

Artistic expression has the power to challenge prevailing narratives, amplify marginalized voices, and inspire social change. Movements like the Harlem Renaissance, feminist art, and protest literature are poignant examples of how art becomes a catalyst for societal transformation.

Education and Cultivation of Creativity:

Recognizing the importance of creativity in fostering well-rounded individuals, education systems worldwide increasingly emphasize the integration of arts into curricula. Arts education not only nurtures the next generation of artists but also equips students with essential skills such as critical thinking, problem-solving, and effective communication.

Engaging with the arts from an early age encourages children to explore their creativity, develop a sense of curiosity, and learn to express themselves authentically. The arts offer a holistic approach to education, fostering emotional intelligence and nurturing skills that are vital in navigating an ever-evolving world.

Art as a Source of Joy and Catharsis:

Beyond its societal and transformative roles, art also serves as a source of joy, inspiration, and catharsis. A beautiful painting, a captivating novel, or a soul-stirring melody has the power to transport individuals to different realms, providing solace and moments of respite.

Artistic endeavors offer creators and audiences alike an opportunity to experience the sublime, transcending the mundane aspects of daily life. The act of creating and appreciating art becomes a form of self-care, a meditative practice that allows individuals to connect with their inner selves and find balance amidst the chaos of the world.

Conclusion:

Art and creativity are inseparable companions on the journey of human expression and exploration. From the earliest cave paintings to the most avant-garde performances, the human impulse to create is a testament to the richness of our inner worlds. Through art, we forge connections, question assumptions, and make sense of the complexity that defines the human experience. In embracing and cultivating creativity, we not only enrich our own lives but contribute to a collective tapestry of innovation, understanding, and shared humanity. Art, in its myriad forms, invites us to embark on a perpetual voyage of discovery—a journey fueled by the boundless potential of the human imagination.

Expressive Arts for Stress Reduction: A Palette of Healing

In the bustling tapestry of modern life, stress has become a near-constant companion for many. Amid the demands of work, relationships, and daily responsibilities, seeking solace through expressive arts has emerged as a powerful and therapeutic outlet. Whether through painting, writing, dance, or music, engaging in expressive arts offers a transformative journey towards stress reduction and emotional well-being.

The Multifaceted Nature of Expressive Arts:

Expressive arts encompass a diverse range of creative modalities, providing individuals with a myriad of ways to channel their emotions and experiences. Painting and drawing allow for visual expression, while writing serves as a literary canvas for introspection. Dance and movement enable the body to communicate, and music becomes a harmonious language for the soul. This multidimensional approach ensures that everyone can find a form of expression that resonates with their innermost selves.

Unleashing Creativity to Alleviate Stress:

The act of creation itself becomes a meditative process, offering a respite from the relentless chatter of the mind. Engaging in expressive arts invites individuals to step into a realm where self-expression takes precedence, and judgment and expectations fade away. This freedom allows for the exploration of emotions, providing a healthy outlet for stressors that may be difficult to articulate verbally.

Painting the Canvas of Emotional Release:

Visual arts, such as painting and drawing, provide a unique avenue for releasing pent-up emotions. The strokes of a brush or the lines on a canvas become a tangible representation of feelings, allowing for externalization and reflection. The act of creating visual art can be both cathartic and empowering, providing a sense of control over one's emotional landscape.

Words as a Gateway to Healing:

Writing, whether in the form of journaling, poetry, or storytelling, serves as a powerful tool for self-discovery and stress relief. The written word has the capacity to untangle complex emotions, offering clarity and insight into one's inner world. By putting thoughts and feelings into words, individuals can navigate through stressors, fostering a sense of release and understanding.

The Rhythmic Dance of Stress Away:

Movement, particularly in the form of dance, is a kinetic expression that transcends verbal communication. The rhythmic dance of the body becomes a metaphor for the ebb and flow of life's challenges. Through dance, individuals can embody and release stress, promoting a sense of liberation and physical well-being.

Harmonizing the Soul with Music:

Music, with its power to evoke emotions, has an unparalleled ability to soothe the soul. Whether through listening to calming melodies or engaging in the creation of music, individuals can tap into a harmonious realm that transcends the cacophony of stress. The rhythmic patterns and melodic tones become a therapeutic symphony for the mind.

The Integrative Approach of Expressive Arts Therapy:

Expressive arts therapy takes a holistic approach, combining various artistic modalities to create a comprehensive healing experience. Therapists guide individuals in using creative expression to explore and process emotions, providing a safe space for self-discovery and stress reduction. This integrative approach recognizes the interconnectedness of mind, body, and spirit in the healing process.

In embracing expressive arts for stress reduction, individuals embark on a personal journey of self-discovery and healing. The act of creation, whether visual, literary, or kinesthetic, becomes a powerful vehicle for transforming stress into a source of empowerment and resilience. As the brush meets the canvas, words flow onto the page, and bodies move to the rhythm, expressive arts offer a palette of healing, inviting individuals to paint their narratives of stress and emerge with a masterpiece of well-being.

Unleashing Creativity as a Form of Self-Care: Nurturing the Soul Through Expression

In the whirlwind of our daily lives, amidst deadlines, responsibilities, and the constant hum of technology, self-care has become an indispensable practice for maintaining mental and emotional well-being. At the intersection of mindfulness and expression lies a powerful form of self-care: unleashing creativity. Engaging in creative endeavors offers a sanctuary for the soul, a space where one can unravel the complexities of emotions, nurture a sense of fulfillment, and cultivate a deep connection with the inner self.

Creativity as a Restorative Force:

Creativity is an innate human quality that often takes a backseat in the hustle and bustle of everyday life. However, it is precisely this capacity to create, whether through art, writing, music, or other forms of expression, that can act as a restorative force. In the act of creating, individuals tap into a reservoir of inspiration that breathes life into their existence, offering a counterbalance to the stresses of the external world.

Mindful Presence in the Creative Process:

Unleashing creativity as a form of self-care is not about producing perfect masterpieces or adhering to external standards; it is about the process itself. The act of creation demands mindful presence, a state where the mind transcends worries about the past or anxieties about the future. In the present moment of creation, individuals find solace, focusing solely on the strokes of a brush, the flow of words, or the melody of a tune.

Artistic Expression as Emotional Release:

The canvas, the page, or the instrument becomes a safe space for emotional release. Through artistic expression, individuals can externalize their inner world, giving form to thoughts and feelings that may be difficult to articulate verbally. This act of catharsis is inherently therapeutic, allowing for the release of pent-up emotions and the cultivation of a more profound understanding of the self.

Fostering a Sense of Fulfillment:

The pursuit of creativity is not bound by external expectations; it is an intrinsically motivated journey that fosters a sense of fulfillment. Whether one is an experienced artist or a novice explorer, the act of creating generates a feeling of accomplishment and joy. The fulfillment derived from the creative process extends beyond the finished product, permeating the very act of engaging with one's imagination and ideas.

Cultivating a Deep Connection Within:

In the quiet moments of creative expression, individuals forge a deep connection with their inner selves. The process of creation is a form of self-discovery, allowing individuals to explore their passions, values, and desires. As one delves into the creative abyss, there is an opportunity to unearth facets of the self that may have remained hidden amidst the demands of daily life.

Integrating Creativity into Daily Self-Care Rituals:

Unleashing creativity as a form of self-care need not be a grand endeavor; it can seamlessly integrate into daily rituals. Whether it's dedicating a few moments to sketching, jotting down thoughts in a journal, or playing an instrument, incorporating creativity into daily life becomes a sustainable and accessible form of self-nurturing.

Conclusion:

In the symphony of self-care practices, unleashing creativity stands out as a melody that resonates with the soul. It is an invitation to dance with imagination, to paint with emotions, and to compose the soundtrack of one's inner world. As individuals embark on the journey of creative self-care, they discover not only the transformative power of artistic expression but also a profound connection with the essence of who they are. In the canvas of creativity, self-care becomes a masterpiece, a testament to the nurturing power of mindful expression in the ongoing journey of well-being.

The Role of Nutrition in Relaxation

Nourishing the Body and Calming the Mind

In the pursuit of relaxation and overall well-being, nutrition plays a pivotal role as a silent yet influential partner. The foods we consume have a direct impact on our physiological and psychological states, influencing our ability to manage stress, unwind, and foster a sense of calmness. Understanding the intricate relationship between nutrition and relaxation unveils a holistic approach to self-care, emphasizing the importance of mindful eating for a tranquil mind and a nourished body.

Balancing Blood Sugar Levels:

One of the fundamental aspects of nutrition for relaxation involves maintaining stable blood sugar levels. Fluctuations in blood sugar can lead to irritability, mood swings, and increased stress levels. To achieve balance, it is advisable to choose complex carbohydrates with a low glycemic index, such as whole grains, legumes, and vegetables. These foods provide a sustained release of energy, preventing the spikes and crashes associated with sugary or processed foods.

The Serotonin Connection:

Serotonin, often referred to as the "feel-good" neurotransmitter, plays a crucial role in mood regulation and relaxation. Certain nutrients, such as tryptophan and complex carbohydrates, contribute to the synthesis of serotonin in the brain. Foods rich in tryptophan include turkey, chicken, dairy products, nuts, and seeds. Incorporating these into the diet can support the body's natural ability to produce serotonin, promoting a sense of calm and well-being.

Magnesium for Muscle Relaxation:

Magnesium is a mineral known for its muscle-relaxing properties. Adequate magnesium levels contribute to the relaxation of smooth muscles, helping to alleviate tension and promote a sense of calmness. Foods rich in magnesium include leafy green vegetables, nuts, seeds, and whole grains. Ensuring an adequate intake of magnesium through diet or supplements can be beneficial for those seeking relaxation and stress reduction.

Adaptogens and Stress Management:

Certain foods, known as adaptogens, have been recognized for their ability to help the body adapt to stress and maintain balance. Examples of adaptogenic foods include ashwagandha, holy basil, and rhodiola. These herbs and roots, often consumed in the form of teas or supplements, have been traditionally used to support the body's stress response and promote relaxation.

Omega-3 Fatty Acids for Brain Health:

Omega-3 fatty acids, found in fatty fish, flaxseeds, chia seeds, and walnuts, play a crucial role in brain health and function. These essential fats contribute to the integrity of cell membranes and support the production of neurotransmitters, including those associated with relaxation. Including sources of omega-3 fatty acids in the diet contributes to overall cognitive well-being and emotional balance.

Hydration and Relaxation:

Proper hydration is a simple yet often overlooked aspect of relaxation. Dehydration can lead to feelings of fatigue, irritability, and difficulty concentrating, all of which contribute to heightened stress levels. Consuming an adequate amount of water throughout the day supports overall well-being and helps maintain physiological balance.

Mindful Eating Practices:

Beyond specific nutrients, the practice of mindful eating itself can contribute to relaxation. Taking the time to savor and appreciate each bite, being present during meals, and paying attention to hunger and fullness cues fosters a mindful relationship with food. This mindful approach enhances the overall dining experience and promotes a sense of calmness and gratitude.

In conclusion, the role of nutrition in relaxation is a multifaceted interplay between the foods we consume and their impact on our physiological and psychological states. By making mindful choices, emphasizing nutrient-dense foods, and recognizing the connection between nutrition and relaxation, individuals can embark on a journey to nourish both body and mind for enhanced well-being.

Mindful Eating for Stress Reduction: Nourishing the Body, Calming the Mind

In the fast-paced rhythm of modern life, where hurried meals and multitasking have become the norm, the practice of mindful eating emerges as a transformative antidote. Mindful eating, rooted in ancient mindfulness traditions, is a conscious and intentional approach to food that not only fosters a healthier relationship with nutrition but also serves as a powerful tool for stress reduction.

The Essence of Mindful Eating:

At its core, mindful eating is about bringing full awareness to the present moment, specifically to the act of eating. It involves engaging all the senses to fully experience the colors, textures, flavors, and aromas of food. By immersing oneself in the sensory experience of eating, individuals can cultivate a profound connection with the nourishment they are providing to their bodies.

Breaking Free from Auto-Pilot Eating:

Often, the daily ritual of eating is marred by distractions – scrolling through smartphones, watching television, or thinking about the next task. Mindful eating invites individuals to break free from auto-pilot eating and instead savor each bite with undivided attention. This intentional focus on the act of eating allows for a richer and more satisfying culinary experience.

Reducing Stress through Mindful Eating:

Cultivating Awareness:

Mindful eating encourages individuals to become attuned to their bodies' hunger and fullness cues. By recognizing these signals, people can respond to their bodies' needs rather than succumbing to external cues or emotional triggers. This awareness contributes to a healthier relationship with food and a reduced likelihood of stress-related overeating.

Embracing the Pleasure of Eating:

Mindful eating encourages individuals to derive pleasure from their meals. By acknowledging and appreciating the flavors and textures of each bite, the act of eating becomes a source of joy rather than a mundane task. This positive association can alleviate stress by fostering a more positive and enjoyable relationship with food.

Preventing Emotional Eating:

Emotional eating, often a response to stress, can be tempered through mindful eating. By staying present and aware during meals, individuals can distinguish between physical hunger and emotional hunger. This awareness empowers them to address emotional needs directly rather than turning to food as a coping mechanism.

Enhancing Digestion:

The mind-body connection is evident in the digestive process. Stress and anxiety can impact digestion negatively. Mindful eating, by promoting relaxation during meals, contributes to improved digestion. Chewing food thoroughly and savoring each bite supports the body's natural digestive functions.

Creating Rituals and Routine:

Establishing mindful eating rituals, such as setting a pleasant dining environment or expressing gratitude before meals, creates a sense of routine and predictability. These rituals can be grounding, providing a moment of calm in the midst of a hectic day.

Practical Tips for Mindful Eating:

- **Eat Without Distractions**: Turn off electronic devices and step away from work while eating.

- **Savor Each Bite:** Take the time to appreciate the flavors, textures, and aromas of your food.

- **Chew Slowly**: Pay attention to the act of chewing. This not only aids digestion but also allows you to be present with your meal.

- **Listen to Your Body**: Tune in to hunger and fullness cues. Eat when hungry, and stop when satisfied.

- **Express Gratitude**: Take a moment to express gratitude for the nourishment your meal provides.

- **Mindful Portion Control**: Be mindful of portion sizes, serving only what you need to satisfy your hunger.

In embracing mindful eating as a practice, individuals not only nourish their bodies with intention but also create a space for stress reduction and a harmonious relationship with food. Mindful eating transforms the simple act of nourishment into a profound and restorative experience, offering a sanctuary of calmness in the midst of life's demands.

Nutritional Strategies for Well-Being

Nutritional strategies play a crucial role in promoting overall well-being by supporting physical health, mental clarity, and emotional balance. Adopting a balanced and nutrient-rich diet can contribute to improved energy levels, enhanced cognitive function, and better emotional resilience. Here are some key nutritional strategies for well-being:

- **Balanced Diet:**

  Aim for a balanced diet that includes a variety of whole foods such as fruits, vegetables, whole grains, lean proteins, and healthy fats. This provides a broad spectrum of essential nutrients, promoting overall health.

- **Hydration:**

  Stay adequately hydrated by consuming an adequate amount of water throughout the day. Dehydration can negatively impact energy levels, cognitive function, and mood.

- **Mindful Eating:**

  Practice mindful eating by paying attention to the sensations of hunger and fullness. Chew your food slowly, savoring each bite, and avoid distractions to promote a healthier relationship with food.

- **Portion Control:**

  Be mindful of portion sizes to avoid overeating. Using smaller plates and listening to your body's hunger and fullness cues can help with portion control.

- **Colorful Plate:**

  Create a colorful plate by incorporating a variety of fruits and vegetables. Different colors often indicate different nutrients, and a diverse range of nutrients supports overall health.

- **Protein-Rich Foods:**

  Include adequate protein in your diet to support muscle health, immune function, and satiety. Sources of lean protein include poultry, fish, beans, lentils, tofu, and dairy products.

- **Healthy Fats:**

  Choose sources of healthy fats, such as avocados, nuts, seeds, and olive oil. These fats are essential for brain health, hormone production, and the absorption of fat-soluble vitamins.

- **Complex Carbohydrates:**

  Prioritize complex carbohydrates, including whole grains, legumes, and starchy vegetables, for sustained energy levels. These foods also provide fiber, which supports digestive health.

- **Limit Processed Foods:**

  Minimize the intake of processed foods, which often contain added sugars, unhealthy fats, and high levels of sodium. Opt for whole, minimally processed foods whenever possible.

- **Omega-3 Fatty Acids:**

  Include sources of omega-3 fatty acids in your diet, such as fatty fish (salmon, mackerel), flaxseeds, chia seeds, and walnuts. Omega-3s support brain health and may have anti-inflammatory effects.

- **Limit Added Sugars:**

  Reduce the consumption of foods and beverages high in added sugars. Excessive sugar intake is linked to various health issues, including obesity and metabolic disorders.

- **Probiotics and Fermented Foods:**

  Incorporate probiotics and fermented foods into your diet to promote a healthy gut microbiome. Yogurt, kefir, sauerkraut, and kimchi are examples of fermented foods that can support digestive health.

- **Vitamin D:**

  Ensure adequate vitamin D intake, either through sunlight exposure or dietary sources like fatty fish, fortified dairy products, and supplements if needed. Vitamin D is essential for bone health and immune function.

- **Mind-Gut Connection:**

  Recognize the connection between the gut and mental well-being. Foods that support gut health, such as fiber-rich foods and fermented products, may positively influence mood and cognitive function.

- **Individualized Approach:**

  Consider individual needs and preferences when planning your diet. What works well for one person may not be suitable for another, so tailor your nutritional choices to your unique requirements.

Remember, these strategies are general guidelines, and individual dietary needs may vary. Consulting with a healthcare professional or a registered dietitian can provide personalized guidance based on specific health conditions, dietary preferences, and goals.

Cultivating a Relaxation Mindset

Nurturing Calmness in the Chaos

In the hustle and bustle of our fast-paced lives, where demands and distractions abound, cultivating a relaxation mindset becomes a powerful antidote to the stressors that often accompany modern living. This mindset is not merely about finding moments of respite but instilling a deeper, sustainable sense of calmness that permeates our daily experiences. By adopting intentional practices and shifting perspectives, individuals can embark on a journey toward cultivating a relaxation mindset that serves as a sanctuary in the midst of life's chaos.

Understanding the Relaxation Mindset:

At its essence, a relaxation mindset involves adopting a conscious and intentional approach to how we perceive and respond to the events and challenges unfolding around us. It goes beyond sporadic moments of relaxation and instead becomes a pervasive lens through which we view our lives. Cultivating this mindset is not about escaping reality but about navigating it with a sense of inner calm and resilience.

Key Components of a Relaxation Mindset:

Mindful Awareness:

The cornerstone of a relaxation mindset is mindful awareness – the ability to be fully present in the current moment without judgment. This involves acknowledging thoughts and feelings without getting entangled in them. Mindfulness practices, such as meditation and mindful breathing, become invaluable tools in fostering this heightened awareness.

Acceptance of Impermanence:

Embracing the idea that life is ever-changing and impermanent is a crucial aspect of cultivating a relaxation mindset. This acceptance allows individuals to navigate challenges with a greater sense of equanimity, knowing that difficulties are transient, and moments of ease will emerge.

Intentional Slow Living:

In a world that often glorifies busyness, intentionally embracing slow living becomes a radical act of self-care. It involves savoring moments, engaging in activities deliberately, and allowing space for rest. The concept of "less is more" becomes a guiding principle in simplifying and finding joy in the present.

Healthy Boundaries:

Establishing and maintaining healthy boundaries is vital for protecting one's mental and emotional well-being. This includes setting limits on work hours, managing digital device use, and being discerning about commitments. Healthy boundaries create a space for relaxation to flourish.

Embracing Self-Compassion:

A relaxation mindset thrives on self-compassion. This involves treating oneself with the same kindness and understanding that would be extended to a friend. Acknowledging one's limitations, celebrating small victories, and embracing self-care rituals are integral to cultivating self-compassion.

Practical Strategies for Cultivating a Relaxation Mindset:

Breath-Centered Practices:

Incorporate regular breath-centered practices into your routine. Techniques such as deep diaphragmatic breathing, mindful breathing, or pranayama can activate the body's relaxation response.

Mindful Breaks:

Take short breaks throughout the day to engage in mindfulness. Whether it's a few minutes of focused breathing, a mindful walk, or a moment of quiet reflection, these breaks can reset your mindset.

Nature Connection:

Spend time in nature to reconnect with the calming influence of the natural world. Whether it's a walk in the park, gardening, or simply sitting by a window, nature has a soothing effect on the mind.

Digital Detox:

Set aside dedicated times for a digital detox. Limit screen time, especially before bedtime, to promote relaxation and better sleep quality.

Journaling:

Engage in reflective journaling to explore thoughts and emotions. This practice provides a space for self-discovery, clarity, and the release of pent-up stress.

Artistic Expression:

Explore artistic forms of expression as a means of relaxation. This could include drawing, painting, writing, or any creative outlet that brings joy and mindfulness.

Gratitude Practice:

Cultivate a gratitude mindset by regularly reflecting on the things you're thankful for. This practice shifts focus toward positive aspects of life, fostering a sense of contentment.

Mindful Eating:

Bring mindfulness to your meals by savoring each bite, appreciating the flavors, and being present during eating. This practice extends the relaxation mindset to daily activities.

The Ripple Effect of a Relaxation Mindset:

As individuals cultivate a relaxation mindset, the benefits extend beyond personal well-being. This mindset ripples into relationships, work, and the broader community. By embodying a sense of calmness and resilience, individuals contribute to creating environments that prioritize mental health, fostering a collective shift toward a more balanced and relaxed way of life.

In the tapestry of daily living, cultivating a relaxation mindset becomes an ongoing practice—a commitment to infusing moments with tranquility and approaching challenges with a grounded and centered presence. It is a transformative journey that invites individuals to rediscover the beauty of simplicity, embrace the ebb and flow of life, and nurture a lasting sense of calmness in the midst of the whirlwind.

Shifting Perspectives on Stress: From Burden to Catalyst for Growth

Stress, often viewed as an unwelcome companion on life's journey, has the potential to be a transformative force when seen through a different lens. Shifting perspectives on stress involves reimagining it not as an insurmountable burden but as a catalyst for personal growth, resilience, and a deeper understanding of oneself. By reframing stress, individuals can harness its energy to propel them forward, fostering a mindset that thrives in the face of life's challenges.

Understanding Stress as a Catalyst:

Inherent Human Experience:

Stress is an inherent aspect of the human experience. Rather than attempting to eliminate it entirely, shifting perspectives involves acknowledging stress as a natural response to life's demands. It becomes a signal that one is engaged, facing challenges, and participating in the dynamic flow of life.

Opportunity for Growth:

Embracing stress as an opportunity for growth reframes adversity as a teacher rather than a threat. The challenges we encounter can serve as stepping stones for personal and professional development, fostering resilience and adaptability.

Building Resilience:

Resilience, the ability to bounce back from adversity, is cultivated through navigating and overcoming stress. Shifting perspectives on stress involves recognizing it as a training ground for resilience, allowing individuals to develop the skills needed to face future challenges with greater ease.

Practical Strategies for Shifting Perspectives:

Mindfulness Practices:

Engage in mindfulness practices to develop awareness of stress triggers and responses. Mindfulness encourages observing stress without judgment, fostering a more objective and empowered perspective.

Cognitive Restructuring:

Challenge and reframe negative thought patterns associated with stress. Identify and replace distorted thinking with more balanced and constructive perspectives, empowering oneself to see challenges as opportunities.

Stress as Motivation:

Channel stress as a source of motivation. Recognize that stress can provide the energy and focus needed to tackle tasks and achieve goals. When viewed as a motivational force, stress becomes a driving factor for accomplishment.

Learning from Adversity:

Approach stressors as opportunities to learn and adapt. Each challenge presents a chance to acquire new skills, insights, and coping mechanisms. Embrace the learning journey that arises from navigating stress.

Cultivating a Growth Mindset:

Develop a growth mindset by viewing challenges as a part of the learning process. Understand that abilities and intelligence can be developed over time, and setbacks are not indicative of permanent limitations.

Balancing Stress and Well-Being:

Self-Care Practices:

Prioritize self-care practices to manage stress effectively. Regular exercise, sufficient sleep, and moments of relaxation contribute to physical and mental well-being, enhancing one's ability to navigate stress.

Seeking Support:

Connect with others and seek support when needed. Sharing experiences and challenges with trusted individuals can provide perspective, encouragement, and a sense of community.

Maintaining Perspective:

Keep stress in perspective by understanding the difference between acute and chronic stress. While acute stress can be motivating, chronic stress requires attention and proactive management to prevent negative health impacts.

Case for Stress as a Catalyst in History:

Throughout history, many individuals have faced seemingly insurmountable challenges and turned them into catalysts for personal and societal transformation. Nelson Mandela, for example, transformed the stress of decades-long imprisonment into a catalyst for forgiveness, reconciliation, and the dismantling of apartheid.

Conclusion

Shifting perspectives on stress involves recognizing it not as an enemy to be avoided but as a dynamic force that, when harnessed thoughtfully, can propel individuals toward greater heights. It's an invitation to view stress as an integral part of the human experience—one that, when navigated with intention and resilience, contributes to a life rich in meaning, growth, and self-discovery. By embracing stress as a catalyst, individuals embark on a journey of empowerment, using challenges as stepping stones toward a more vibrant and fulfilling existence.

Embracing Relaxation as a Lifestyle: Crafting a Serene Tapestry of Well-Being

In the midst of the whirlwind of modern life, where constant connectivity and ever-increasing demands can leave individuals feeling stretched thin, the notion of embracing relaxation as a lifestyle emerges as a transformative choice. It involves not merely seeking occasional respites but consciously weaving relaxation into the fabric of one's daily existence—a commitment to cultivating a serene and balanced way of living that prioritizes well-being. Embracing relaxation as a lifestyle is an intentional journey that unfolds as individuals craft a tapestry of calmness amidst life's complexities.

Defining Relaxation as a Lifestyle:

Holistic Well-Being:

Embracing relaxation as a lifestyle transcends viewing it as a brief escape from stress. It encompasses a commitment to holistic well-being—nurturing mental, emotional, and physical health in harmony. It becomes a conscious choice to integrate relaxation into various aspects of life, from work to relationships to personal pursuits.

Mindful Presence:

At its core, a lifestyle of relaxation is rooted in mindful presence. It involves being fully engaged in the present moment, appreciating the nuances of everyday experiences, and intentionally creating space for tranquility. This mindful approach extends beyond designated relaxation times to permeate the entirety of one's day.

Key Components of a Relaxed Lifestyle:

Mindful Practices:

Incorporate mindfulness practices into daily life. Whether through meditation, mindful breathing, or simply being present during routine activities, these practices anchor individuals in the present moment, fostering a sense of calm.

Healthy Work-Life Integration:

Reimagine the relationship between work and leisure. Strive for a healthy integration of work and personal life, setting boundaries to prevent burnout and allowing time for rest and rejuvenation.

Prioritizing Sleep:

Recognize the importance of quality sleep in maintaining overall well-being. Prioritize sleep hygiene, create a restful bedtime routine, and ensure sufficient hours of sleep to support physical and mental health.

Nourishing Nutrition:

Embrace a balanced and nourishing approach to nutrition. Consume foods that support energy levels and well-being, and cultivate mindful eating practices that enhance the enjoyment of meals.

Nature Connection:

Infuse nature into daily life. Whether through walks in the park, tending to a garden, or simply spending time outdoors, nature connection provides a natural source of tranquility.

Digital Detox:

Integrate periods of digital detox into the routine. Limit screen time, especially before bedtime, to create space for relaxation and reduce the impact of constant digital stimuli.

Creative Expression:

Engage in creative pursuits that bring joy and relaxation. Whether it's art, writing, music, or any form of self-expression, creativity becomes a channel for relaxation and self-discovery.

Meaningful Connections:

Cultivate meaningful connections with others. Prioritize quality relationships, invest time in nurturing connections, and create a support system that contributes to emotional well-being.

The Transformative Power of a Relaxed Lifestyle:

Enhanced Resilience:

A lifestyle centered around relaxation fosters resilience in the face of challenges. By consistently nurturing well-being, individuals develop the inner strength to navigate stressors with greater ease.

Heightened Awareness:

Mindful living cultivates heightened awareness. Individuals become attuned to their thoughts, emotions, and the impact of their choices, fostering a deeper understanding of themselves and their needs.

Joy in the Simple Moments:

Embracing relaxation as a lifestyle allows individuals to find joy in simple moments. The appreciation of everyday experiences becomes a source of fulfillment, contributing to a more positive and contented outlook.

Balanced Energy:

Rather than succumbing to constant busyness and energy depletion, a relaxed lifestyle promotes balanced energy. It involves recognizing the rhythms of productivity and rest, allowing for sustained well-being.

Navigating Challenges:

While embracing relaxation as a lifestyle is transformative, it doesn't negate life's inevitable challenges. Instead, it equips individuals with the tools and mindset to navigate challenges with resilience and grace. The ability to return to a centered and relaxed state becomes a valuable asset in facing the ebb and flow of life.

Conclusion:

In the grand tapestry of life, the choice to embrace relaxation as a lifestyle is an ongoing commitment—a daily weaving of threads that create a serene and harmonious existence. It's an intentional journey where individuals prioritize well-being, savor the richness of each moment, and consciously craft a life that resonates with tranquility. Ultimately, the embrace of relaxation as a lifestyle is an invitation to live fully, authentically, and in alignment with the calm rhythm of one's own being.

Self-Care Rituals

Nurturing Your Well-Being with Intentional Practices

In the whirlwind of daily life, where responsibilities, deadlines, and demands often take center stage, the concept of self-care emerges as a sanctuary—a deliberate and compassionate act of prioritizing one's own well-being. Self-care goes beyond sporadic indulgences; it involves the cultivation of rituals, intentional practices woven into the fabric of daily life that nourish the body, mind, and spirit. These rituals become anchors of stability, fostering resilience and a deeper connection with oneself.

Defining Self-Care Rituals:

Intentional Practices:

Self-care rituals are intentional and purposeful practices designed to promote well-being. They are not haphazard activities but deliberate choices that honor and nurture the multifaceted aspects of one's being.

Consistency and Rhythm:

Unlike occasional acts of self-indulgence, self-care rituals thrive on consistency and rhythm. They become an integral part of daily, weekly, or monthly routines, creating a dependable structure that supports overall well-being.

Key Elements of Self-Care Rituals:

Mindfulness:

At the heart of self-care rituals lies mindfulness—the art of being fully present in the current moment. Whether it's a quiet moment of reflection, a soothing cup of tea, or a gentle yoga session, mindfulness infuses each ritual with a sense of awareness and presence.

Holistic Well-Being:

Self-care rituals address holistic well-being, considering the interconnectedness of the body, mind, and spirit. They encompass practices that nourish physical health, nurture emotional resilience, and foster mental clarity.

Individualized and Personal:

Self-care is a deeply personal journey. Rituals are tailored to individual preferences, needs, and values. What brings solace and rejuvenation to one person may differ from another, highlighting the importance of personalized self-care practices.

Joyful and Nurturing:

Effective self-care rituals are infused with joy and a sense of nurturing. Whether it's engaging in a beloved hobby, spending time in nature, or enjoying a favorite book, these rituals bring forth positive emotions and a deep sense of replenishment.

Examples of Self-Care Rituals:

Morning Mindfulness Routine:

Begin the day with a mindful ritual, such as deep breathing exercises, meditation, or a few moments of gratitude. Setting a positive tone in the morning can influence the rest of the day.

Digital Detox Evenings:

Dedicate a specific time each evening to a digital detox. Turn off electronic devices, disconnect from screens, and engage in activities that promote relaxation, such as reading, gentle stretching, or enjoying a warm bath.

Nature Connection:

Incorporate rituals that involve connecting with nature, whether it's a daily walk in a nearby park, gardening, or simply sitting in a green space. Nature has a rejuvenating effect on mental and emotional well-being.

Sensory Delights:

Create rituals that engage the senses. This could involve lighting scented candles, indulging in aromatherapy, or enjoying a mindful meal that delights the taste buds.

Reflective Journaling:

Set aside time for reflective journaling, allowing thoughts and emotions to flow onto paper. This practice promotes self-awareness, clarity, and the release of pent-up stress.

Creative Expression:

Embrace creative self-care rituals, such as drawing, writing, or playing a musical instrument. Creative expression provides an outlet for emotions and fosters a sense of fulfillment.

Restorative Sleep Practices:

Establish a bedtime ritual that promotes restorative sleep. This may include activities like reading a calming book, practicing gentle stretches, or engaging in a short meditation before bedtime.

The Impact of Consistent Self-Care Rituals:

Enhanced Resilience:

Regular self-care rituals contribute to enhanced resilience in the face of life's challenges. They provide a foundation of support that helps individuals navigate stress with greater ease.

Improved Mental Health:

Consistent self-care rituals are linked to improved mental health. They offer moments of respite, reduce the impact of daily stressors, and contribute to a more positive mindset.

Balanced Energy Levels:

Self-care rituals contribute to balanced energy levels by recognizing the need for rest and rejuvenation. They prevent burnout and support sustained well-being.

Deepened Self-Connection:

Engaging in intentional self-care rituals fosters a deepened connection with oneself. It creates a space for self-reflection, self-compassion, and an understanding of one's needs and desires.

Conclusion:

In the tapestry of a well-lived life, self-care rituals are the threads that weave together moments of solace, joy, and rejuvenation. They are not mere luxuries but essential practices that contribute to a life infused with intention, resilience, and a profound sense of self-compassion. By embracing self-care as a lifestyle, individuals cultivate a sanctuary within, fostering a well-nurtured and flourishing existence.

Building Personalized Self-Care Practices: Crafting a Well-Being Blueprint

In the journey of life, where the demands of work, relationships, and personal growth often take precedence, the cultivation of personalized self-care practices emerges as a transformative and empowering endeavor. Unlike generic self-care routines, personalized practices are tailored to an individual's unique needs, preferences, and lifestyle. They become a well-being blueprint, guiding individuals toward intentional choices that nurture their physical, emotional, and mental health. Building personalized self-care practices is a journey of self-discovery and self-compassion, inviting individuals to craft a sustainable and fulfilling approach to well-being.

Understanding Personalized Self-Care:

Tailored to Individual Needs:

Personalized self-care practices are precisely that—personal. They are designed to meet the specific needs of an individual, considering factors such as personality, preferences, energy levels, and even the ebb and flow of life.

Holistic Approach:

Unlike one-size-fits-all approaches, personalized self-care adopts a holistic perspective. It recognizes that well-being is interconnected, addressing physical, emotional, and mental aspects of health in a harmonious manner.

Steps to Build Personalized Self-Care Practices:

Self-Reflection:

Begin by reflecting on your current well-being and identifying areas that need attention. Consider aspects of your life that bring joy, stressors that impact you, and activities that rejuvenate you.

Identify Core Values:

Define your core values and priorities. What matters most to you in life? Understanding your values guides the creation of self-care practices aligned with your aspirations and principles.

Assess Energy Levels:

Take stock of your energy levels throughout the day and week. Identify times when you feel most energized and times when you need rest. Build self-care practices that align with your natural rhythms.

Explore Interests and Hobbies:

Consider activities that genuinely interest and engage you. Whether it's a creative pursuit, physical activity, or time spent in nature, incorporating hobbies into self-care practices adds a layer of joy and fulfillment.

Customize for Your Lifestyle:

Personalized self-care practices must fit seamlessly into your lifestyle. Consider practicalities such as work commitments, family responsibilities, and daily routines. Build practices that are realistic and sustainable.

Examples of Personalized Self-Care Practices:

Mindful Morning Routine:

Tailor a morning routine that aligns with your preferences. It could include elements like meditation, gentle stretches, or a mindful cup of tea. The key is to start the day in a way that resonates with you.

Digital Detox:

Design a personalized digital detox plan. Identify specific times or days when you disconnect from screens, allowing yourself to be present in the offline world and reducing the impact of constant digital stimuli.

Nature Connection:

If you're drawn to nature, build self-care practices that involve spending time outdoors. It could be a weekly hike, gardening, or simply taking a mindful walk in a nearby park.

Creative Expression:

Explore creative outlets that speak to your soul. Whether it's painting, writing, or playing a musical instrument, personalized self-care practices can include regular sessions of creative expression.

Restorative Sleep Rituals:

Customize your bedtime routine to promote restorative sleep. This might involve calming activities such as reading a book, practicing relaxation exercises, or creating a soothing ambiance in your sleep environment.

The Impact of Personalized Self-Care:

Increased Satisfaction:

Personalized self-care practices lead to increased satisfaction as they align with your values and preferences. Engaging in activities that resonate with you brings a sense of fulfillment and purpose.

Enhanced Well-Being:

By addressing your unique needs, personalized self-care practices contribute to enhanced overall well-being. They become a proactive approach to maintaining physical health, emotional resilience, and mental clarity.

Sustainable Habits:

Because personalized self-care practices are tailored to your lifestyle, they are more likely to become sustainable habits. When self-care aligns with your routine and interests, it seamlessly integrates into your daily life.

Stress Reduction:

Personalized self-care acts as a powerful stress reduction tool. Engaging in activities that bring joy and relaxation helps manage stress and prevents burnout, promoting a balanced and healthy life.

Conclusion:

Building personalized self-care practices is an ongoing journey of self-discovery, intention, and self-compassion. It's an acknowledgment that your well-being is unique and deserves tailored attention. By crafting a well-being blueprint that reflects your values and resonates with your individuality, you embark on a path of sustained health, joy, and fulfillment—one that honors the intricate tapestry of your life.

Creating a Self-Care Routine: Cultivating a Ritual of Well-Being

In the hustle and bustle of daily life, where responsibilities often take center stage, the creation of a self-care routine emerges as a transformative practice—an intentional commitment to prioritize well-being amid the myriad demands. Unlike sporadic acts of self-indulgence, a self-care routine is a structured and consistent set of practices designed to nurture the body, mind, and spirit. It becomes a ritual of well-being, a sanctuary that individuals carve out for themselves to foster resilience, balance, and a deep sense of self-compassion.

Defining a Self-Care Routine:

Structured and Consistent:

A self-care routine is structured and consistent, involving a set of intentional practices incorporated into daily, weekly, or monthly schedules. It thrives on regularity, providing a dependable framework for well-being.

Holistic Approach:

Unlike isolated acts of self-care, a routine adopts a holistic perspective. It encompasses practices that address physical health, emotional well-being, and mental clarity, recognizing the interconnectedness of these facets.

Steps to Create a Self-Care Routine:

Self-Reflection:

Begin by reflecting on your current well-being. Identify areas of your life that could benefit from intentional care and attention. Consider stressors, energy levels, and activities that bring you joy and relaxation.

Identify Priorities:

Determine your priorities and values. What aspects of your life are most important to you? Align your self-care routine with these priorities to ensure it is meaningful and fulfilling.

Start Small:

Begin with small, manageable steps. Overcommitting can lead to frustration and abandonment of the routine. Start with a few practices that are realistic and achievable within your current lifestyle.

Experiment and Adapt:

Treat the creation of your routine as an experiment. Try different practices and pay attention to what resonates with you. Be open to adaptation, allowing your routine to evolve based on your needs and preferences.

Components of a Self-Care Routine:

Mindful Mornings:

Start your day with intention. Incorporate activities such as meditation, deep breathing exercises, or a moment of gratitude to set a positive tone for the day.

Digital Detox:

Designate specific times for a digital detox. Disconnect from screens to reduce the impact of constant digital stimuli and create space for relaxation.

Physical Well-Being:

Include activities that support physical health. This could involve regular exercise, stretching, or engaging in activities that bring joy and vitality to your body.

Restorative Sleep Practices:

Develop a bedtime routine that promotes restorative sleep. Create a calming environment, engage in relaxing activities, and prioritize sufficient hours of sleep.

Creative Expression:

Incorporate creative outlets into your routine. Whether it's writing, drawing, or playing a musical instrument, creative expression contributes to emotional well-being.

Nature Connection:

Spend time in nature. Whether it's a daily walk, gardening, or simply enjoying the outdoors, nature connection has a rejuvenating effect.

Reflective Journaling:

Set aside time for reflective journaling. Capture your thoughts, emotions, and reflections, promoting self-awareness and clarity.

Benefits of a Self-Care Routine:

Stress Reduction:

A well-crafted self-care routine acts as a powerful tool for stress reduction. Engaging in activities that promote relaxation and joy helps manage stress and prevent burnout.

Enhanced Well-Being:

Consistent self-care practices contribute to enhanced overall well-being. They support physical health, emotional resilience, and mental clarity, fostering a balanced and healthy life.

Routine as a Source of Comfort:

A structured routine becomes a source of comfort and stability in the midst of life's uncertainties. Knowing that there are dedicated moments for self-care provides a sense of security.

Increased Resilience:

Regular self-care practices build resilience. They equip individuals with the tools to navigate challenges with greater ease, fostering a mindset of adaptability and strength.

Conclusion:

Creating a self-care routine is an act of self-love and empowerment. It's a commitment to prioritize your well-being and cultivate a sanctuary of care amid life's demands. By weaving intentional practices into your daily rhythm, you embark on a journey of sustained health, balance, and a profound sense of self-compassion—a journey that honors the importance of nurturing yourself in the midst of life's beautiful chaos.

Connecting with Nature

Nurturing Well-Being Through Earth's Embrace

In the modern hustle and bustle of urban life, amidst towering skyscrapers and bustling streets, the call to connect with nature reverberates as a beckoning whisper—a reminder of our intrinsic bond with the Earth and the rejuvenating embrace it offers. Connecting with nature transcends mere leisure; it is a profound practice of grounding, healing, and reawakening our innate connection to the natural world. From tranquil forests to vast oceans, from sun-kissed meadows to majestic mountains, nature beckons us to rediscover our roots, replenish our spirits, and find solace in its timeless embrace.

The Essence of Connecting with Nature:

At its core, connecting with nature is about rekindling our relationship with the Earth. It is a recognition of our interconnectedness with all living beings and the ecosystems that sustain life.

Mindful Presence:

Connecting with nature invites us to be fully present in the moment, to engage our senses, and to immerse ourselves in the beauty and wonder that surrounds us. It is a practice of mindful awareness, where each rustle of leaves, each chirp of a bird, becomes a symphony of serenity.

The Healing Power of Nature:

Stress Reduction and Relaxation:

Nature has a remarkable ability to soothe the mind and body, offering respite from the stresses of daily life. Studies have shown that spending time in natural environments can reduce cortisol levels, lower blood pressure, and promote relaxation.

Emotional Well-Being:

Nature has a profound impact on emotional well-being, offering solace during times of sadness or anxiety. The beauty of natural landscapes can evoke feelings of awe, gratitude, and connectedness, lifting the spirits and nurturing the soul.

Physical Health Benefits:

Engaging with nature often involves physical activity, whether it's hiking through forests, swimming in lakes, or simply walking along the beach. These activities promote physical health, improving cardiovascular fitness, boosting immune function, and enhancing overall well-being.

Ways to Connect with Nature:

Immersive Wilderness Adventures:

Venture into the wilderness and explore untouched landscapes. Whether it's backpacking through rugged mountains, kayaking along pristine rivers, or camping beneath starlit skies, immersive wilderness adventures offer an opportunity to disconnect from the chaos of civilization and reconnect with the rhythms of nature.

Forest Bathing:

Practice Shinrin-yoku, or forest bathing, a Japanese tradition that involves immersing oneself in the sights, sounds, and scents of the forest. Simply being present in a wooded area, breathing in the phytoncides released by trees, can have profound calming and rejuvenating effects on the mind and body.

Gardening and Horticulture:

Cultivate a connection with nature close to home by tending to a garden or engaging in horticultural activities. Digging in the soil, planting seeds, and nurturing plants not only fosters a sense of responsibility and care but also provides an opportunity to witness the wonders of growth and renewal firsthand.

Nature Walks and Birdwatching:

Take leisurely strolls through parks, nature reserves, or botanical gardens, observing the beauty of flora and fauna. Birdwatching, in particular, offers a chance to connect with the avian world, sharpening observation skills and fostering appreciation for the delicate balance of ecosystems.

Sunrise and Sunset Contemplation:

Witness the awe-inspiring beauty of sunrise and sunset, moments when the sky is painted in hues of gold, pink, and violet. Whether it's atop a mountain peak, by the ocean's edge, or in the comfort of your backyard, these fleeting moments remind us of the cyclical nature of life and the promise of new beginnings.

The Transformative Impact:

Cultivating Awe and Gratitude:

Connecting with nature cultivates feelings of awe and gratitude, fostering a deeper appreciation for the beauty and complexity of the natural world. These emotions can shift perspective, reminding us of the profound interconnectedness of all life and our place within it.

Inspiration and Creativity:

Nature serves as a wellspring of inspiration for artists, writers, and creatives, igniting the imagination and fueling creativity. Whether it's capturing the play of light on water, the intricate patterns of a leaf, or the majesty of a mountain vista, nature's beauty inspires works of art that reflect the splendor of the world around us.

Environmental Stewardship:

A deep connection with nature often leads to a sense of responsibility and stewardship for the environment. As individuals experience the wonder and fragility of natural ecosystems, they are motivated to protect and preserve these precious resources for future generations.

Conclusion:

In a world characterized by rapid urbanization and technological advancement, the importance of connecting with nature has never been more profound. It is a practice of reconnection, healing, and rejuvenation—a return to our roots and a rediscovery of the timeless wisdom inherent in the natural world. By immersing ourselves in the beauty and wonder of nature, we nourish our bodies, rejuvenate our spirits, and cultivate a deep sense of belonging to the intricate web of life that sustains us all.

The Healing Power of Nature: Embracing Earth's Restorative Touch

Nature, with its boundless beauty and innate serenity, possesses a profound capacity to heal and nurture the human spirit. In the gentle rustle of leaves, the rhythmic lapping of waves, and the vibrant hues of a sunset, lies a timeless invitation to find solace, renewal, and restoration. From ancient traditions to modern scientific research, the healing power of nature has been celebrated and validated, offering a sanctuary for weary souls seeking refuge from the stresses of daily life.

The Essence of Healing in Nature:

A Source of Calm and Serenity:

Nature's tranquil landscapes and rhythmic cycles evoke a sense of calm and serenity, providing a respite from the frenetic pace of modern living. The gentle sway of trees, the soft murmur of streams, and the vast expanse of starlit skies envelop individuals in a comforting embrace, soothing frayed nerves and quieting restless minds.

Promoting Mindful Awareness:

Immersed in nature's embrace, individuals are invited to cultivate mindful awareness, anchoring themselves in the present moment. Whether it's the intricate patterns of a leaf, the delicate fragrance of wildflowers, or the playful dance of sunlight through branches, nature captivates the senses, drawing individuals into a state of heightened awareness and appreciation.

The Healing Benefits of Nature:

Stress Reduction and Relaxation:

Numerous studies have demonstrated nature's ability to reduce stress levels and promote relaxation. Time spent in natural environments has been linked to lower cortisol levels, decreased heart rate, and enhanced feelings of tranquility, offering a natural antidote to the pressures of modern life.

Mental Health and Emotional Well-Being:

Nature serves as a sanctuary for emotional healing and resilience. Immersion in natural settings has been shown to alleviate symptoms of anxiety, depression, and mood disorders, fostering a sense of emotional balance and well-being. The beauty and tranquility of nature evoke feelings of awe, gratitude, and connectedness, lifting spirits and nurturing the soul.

Physical Health Benefits:

Engaging with nature often involves physical activity, whether it's hiking through forests, swimming in lakes, or simply walking along the beach. These activities promote physical health, improving cardiovascular fitness, boosting immune function, and enhancing overall well-being.

Ways to Embrace Nature's Healing Touch:

Forest Therapy and Shinrin-Yoku:

Forest therapy, inspired by the Japanese practice of Shinrin-Yoku or "forest bathing," involves immersing oneself in the healing atmosphere of the forest. Guided forest therapy sessions encourage participants to engage their senses, connecting with nature in a deeply experiential way.

Water Therapy and Coastal Retreats:

Water therapy harnesses the restorative power of oceans, rivers, and lakes. Coastal retreats offer opportunities for relaxation, rejuvenation, and reflection, with the rhythmic ebb and flow of tides serving as a soothing backdrop.

Gardening and Horticultural Therapy:

Gardening provides a therapeutic outlet for connecting with nature and nurturing plant life. Horticultural therapy programs leverage gardening activities to promote physical, emotional, and social well-being, fostering a sense of purpose and accomplishment.

Conclusion:

In the bustling cacophony of modern life, nature stands as a timeless sanctuary—a healing balm for body, mind, and soul. Its restorative touch offers solace, renewal, and inspiration, inviting individuals to reconnect with the rhythms of the Earth and rediscover the innate wisdom of the natural world. As we heed nature's call and embrace its healing power, we embark on a journey of profound transformation—a journey guided by the gentle whispers of wind, the murmurs of streams, and the silent symphony of stars, leading us back to the essence of our true selves.

Outdoor Activities for Relaxation: Embracing Nature's Tranquil Haven

Outdoor activities offer a gateway to the natural world, inviting individuals to immerse themselves in the beauty and tranquility of the great outdoors. From serene forest hikes to leisurely strolls along sun-kissed beaches, these experiences provide a therapeutic escape from the stresses of daily life. Engaging in outdoor activities not only promotes physical well-being but also nurtures mental clarity, emotional resilience, and spiritual renewal. Here are several examples of outdoor activities specifically designed to foster relaxation:

Forest Bathing (Shinrin-Yoku):

Forest bathing, inspired by the Japanese practice of Shinrin-Yoku, involves immersing oneself in the therapeutic atmosphere of the forest. Participants are encouraged to engage their senses fully, taking in the sights, sounds, and scents of the woodland environment. A leisurely stroll through a lush forest, pausing to observe the intricate details of flora and fauna, can evoke a profound sense of peace and connection with nature.

Beach Meditation and Sunset Watching:

Visiting the beach offers a serene backdrop for meditation and mindfulness practices. As the rhythmic sound of waves lulls the mind into a state of tranquility, individuals can find solace in the vast expanse of the ocean and the breathtaking beauty of a sunset. Sitting in quiet contemplation as the sun dips below the horizon, casting a golden glow over the water, can be a deeply meditative and rejuvenating experience.

Nature Walks and Birdwatching:

Taking leisurely walks through natural landscapes, such as parks, nature reserves, or botanical gardens, allows individuals to reconnect with the rhythms of the Earth. Observing the diverse flora and fauna, listening to birdsong, and feeling the gentle caress of a breeze against the skin can foster a profound sense of calm and wonder. Birdwatching, in particular, offers an opportunity to hone observation skills and deepen appreciation for the avian world.

Yoga and Tai Chi in Nature:

Practicing yoga or Tai Chi in outdoor settings amplifies the restorative benefits of these ancient disciplines. Whether it's a sun salutation on a grassy meadow or a series of Tai Chi movements by a tranquil lake, the natural surroundings enhance the sense of connection with the Earth and facilitate a deeper sense of relaxation and mindfulness.

Picnics and Nature Retreats:

Planning a picnic in a scenic outdoor location provides an opportunity to unwind and savor the simple pleasures of life. Whether it's a family outing in a local park or a romantic rendezvous in a secluded meadow, sharing a meal amidst nature's beauty fosters bonds of camaraderie and renews the spirit.

Kayaking or Canoeing on Calm Waters:

Paddling along serene lakes, rivers, or estuaries offers a tranquil escape from the hustle and bustle of urban life. The rhythmic motion of paddling, coupled with the soothing sounds of water lapping against the boat, induces a meditative state conducive to relaxation and introspection.

Stargazing and Nighttime Nature Walks:

Exploring the wonders of the night sky, far from the glare of city lights, can be a mesmerizing and awe-inspiring experience. Whether it's identifying constellations, watching for shooting stars, or simply marveling at the vastness of the universe, stargazing reconnects individuals with the cosmic rhythms of the cosmos, instilling a sense of wonder and humility.

Incorporating these outdoor activities into one's routine provides a gateway to holistic well-being, fostering a deeper connection with nature and nurturing the body, mind, and soul. By embracing the restorative power of the great outdoors, individuals can cultivate a sense of inner peace, resilience, and vitality, finding solace and rejuvenation amidst the natural beauty that surrounds them.

Social Connection and Support

Nurturing Bonds for Well-Being

In the intricate tapestry of human existence, social connection serves as a fundamental thread—a source of comfort, companionship, and belonging that enriches our lives and sustains our well-being. From shared laughter with friends to heartfelt conversations with loved ones, the bonds we forge with others provide a vital lifeline, offering support during times of joy, sorrow, and everything in between. As social beings, our need for connection is deeply ingrained, influencing our mental, emotional, and physical health in profound ways.

The Importance of Social Connection:

Emotional Resilience:

Social connections act as a buffer against stress and adversity, providing emotional support and encouragement during challenging times. Strong social ties foster resilience, helping individuals navigate life's ups and downs with greater ease and grace.

Mental Well-Being:

Meaningful social relationships contribute to positive mental health outcomes, reducing the risk of depression, anxiety, and loneliness. Regular social interactions stimulate the release of neurotransmitters such as dopamine and oxytocin, promoting feelings of happiness, trust, and relaxation.

Physical Health Benefits:

Research has shown that strong social support networks are associated with better physical health outcomes and longevity. Close relationships and social connections have been linked to lower rates of chronic diseases, improved immune function, and faster recovery from illness or injury.

Types of Social Support:

Emotional Support:

Emotional support involves empathetic listening, validation of feelings, and expressions of care and concern. It provides comfort and reassurance during times of distress, helping individuals feel understood, accepted, and valued.

Instrumental Support:

Instrumental support entails tangible assistance, such as practical help with tasks or financial support during times of need. Whether it's offering a helping hand with household chores, providing transportation to appointments, or lending a financial helping hand, instrumental support addresses practical needs and alleviates burdens.

Informational Support:

Informational support involves the provision of advice, guidance, and information to help individuals navigate challenges and make informed decisions. Whether it's seeking guidance from a mentor, consulting with a trusted friend, or accessing resources online, informational support empowers individuals to address problems and overcome obstacles.

Cultivating Social Connections:

Nurture Existing Relationships:

Invest time and effort in nurturing existing relationships with family, friends, and acquaintances. Reach out regularly through phone calls, text messages, or in-person visits to maintain connections and strengthen bonds.

Participate in Group Activities:

Engage in group activities or shared interests that facilitate social interaction and connection. Join clubs, community organizations, or recreational sports teams to meet new people and expand your social network.

Practice Active Listening:

Be present and attentive during conversations, practicing active listening and empathy. Show genuine interest in others' experiences, perspectives, and emotions, fostering deeper connections and understanding.

Seek Support When Needed:

Don't hesitate to reach out for support when facing challenges or experiencing distress. Whether it's confiding in a trusted friend, seeking guidance from a counselor, or attending support groups, reaching out for help is a sign of strength, not weakness.

Conclusion:

Social connection is a cornerstone of human experience—a source of strength, comfort, and joy that enriches our lives in countless ways. By nurturing meaningful relationships, offering support to others, and seeking support when needed, we cultivate a sense of belonging and resilience that sustains us through life's journey. As we embrace the power of social connection, we create a ripple effect of compassion, empathy, and solidarity that uplifts us individually and strengthens our communities as a whole.

The Role of Relationships in Stress Reduction: Building Bridges to Resilience

In the intricate dance of life, relationships serve as both anchors and sails, guiding us through calm waters and turbulent seas alike. Our connections with family, friends, colleagues, and community members play a pivotal role in shaping our experiences and influencing our ability to navigate stress and adversity. By fostering supportive, nurturing relationships, individuals can cultivate a sense of belonging, security, and resilience that buffers against the negative effects of stress and promotes overall well-being.

1. Emotional Support:

Relationships provide a vital source of emotional support during times of stress and hardship. Trusted friends, family members, and loved ones offer a listening ear, a shoulder to lean on, and words of encouragement that validate our feelings and experiences. Knowing that we are not alone in our struggles and that others care about our well-being can alleviate feelings of isolation and helplessness, empowering us to face challenges with greater courage and determination.

2. Social Connection:

Engaging in meaningful social interactions fosters a sense of connection and belonging that is essential for emotional well-being. Spending time with friends, participating in group activities, and attending social gatherings provide opportunities for laughter, camaraderie, and shared experiences that uplift the spirit and promote a sense of community. These connections remind us that we are part of something larger than ourselves, instilling a sense of purpose and meaning in our lives that transcends individual stressors.

3. Stress Buffering Effect:

Strong, supportive relationships act as a buffer against the negative effects of stress, helping individuals cope more effectively with life's challenges. Research has shown that individuals with close social ties experience lower levels of stress hormones, such as cortisol, and exhibit greater resilience in the face of adversity. The emotional reassurance and practical assistance provided by supportive relationships help individuals weather storms with grace and resilience, minimizing the impact of stress on their physical and mental well-being.

4. Shared Coping Strategies:

Relationships offer a platform for shared coping strategies and problem-solving techniques that enhance resilience and adaptive functioning. Collaborating with others to identify solutions, brainstorm ideas, and implement action plans fosters a sense of agency and empowerment that strengthens individuals' ability to navigate stressful situations. Whether it's seeking advice from a trusted friend, brainstorming solutions with a supportive partner, or participating in group therapy sessions, shared coping strategies harness the collective wisdom and resources of the community to promote effective stress management and resolution.

5. Mutual Support and Reciprocity:

Healthy relationships are characterized by mutual support and reciprocity, where individuals give and receive help, encouragement, and care in equal measure. By nurturing reciprocal relationships built on trust, respect, and empathy, individuals create a supportive network of allies who are there to offer assistance and encouragement when needed. This mutual support system bolsters resilience, fosters a sense of belonging, and strengthens social bonds that endure through life's challenges.

Conclusion:

In the tapestry of human experience, relationships form the fabric that binds us together, offering solace, strength, and support during times of stress and uncertainty. By cultivating meaningful connections with others, individuals can harness the power of social support to navigate life's challenges with grace and resilience. Whether through emotional reassurance, social connection, shared coping strategies, or mutual support, relationships serve as potent antidotes to the corrosive effects of stress, building bridges to resilience and fostering a sense of hope, connection, and belonging in our lives.

Building a Supportive Social Network: Strengthening Connections for Resilience

In the intricate tapestry of human experience, our social networks serve as the threads that bind us together, weaving a web of support, companionship, and belonging that sustains us through life's ups and downs. Building and nurturing a supportive social network is essential for cultivating resilience, fostering emotional well-being, and navigating the challenges of daily life with grace and fortitude. By investing in meaningful connections with family, friends, colleagues, and community members, individuals can create a robust support system that enriches their lives and bolsters their ability to thrive in the face of adversity.

1. Identify Your Social Circle:

Start by identifying the individuals in your life who play a supportive role and bring positivity, encouragement, and understanding into your world. This may include family members, close friends, coworkers, neighbors, mentors, and members of community groups or organizations with shared interests.

2. Nurture Existing Relationships:

Invest time and effort in nurturing existing relationships, cultivating a sense of trust, reciprocity, and mutual respect. Reach out regularly to maintain connections, whether through phone calls, text messages, or in-person visits. Make an effort to listen attentively, show empathy, and express appreciation for the role each person plays in your life.

3. Expand Your Social Circle:

Seek out opportunities to expand your social circle and meet new people who share your interests, values, and goals. Join clubs, organizations, or hobby groups where you can connect with like-minded individuals and forge new friendships. Attend networking events, workshops, or social gatherings where you can meet people from diverse backgrounds and perspectives.

4. Foster Authentic Connections:

Prioritize authenticity and vulnerability in your interactions, sharing your thoughts, feelings, and experiences openly and honestly. Be willing to listen to others with empathy and compassion, offering support and encouragement without judgment or criticism. Authentic connections are built on trust and authenticity, creating a safe space for individuals to express themselves authentically and feel accepted for who they are.

5. Be Proactive in Seeking Support:

Don't hesitate to reach out for support when needed, whether it's for practical assistance, emotional encouragement, or a listening ear. Be proactive in communicating your needs and asking for help when you're feeling overwhelmed or struggling with challenges. Remember that seeking support is a sign of strength, not weakness, and that most people are willing to offer help when asked.

6. Cultivate Reciprocal Relationships:

Strive to cultivate reciprocal relationships built on mutual support, respect, and trust. Offer assistance, encouragement, and kindness to others in your social network, knowing that your actions will be reciprocated when you need support in return. Building reciprocal relationships creates a sense of interconnectedness and shared responsibility, strengthening the bonds of friendship and community.

7. Embrace Diverse Perspectives:

Embrace diversity within your social network, seeking out connections with individuals from different backgrounds, cultures, and life experiences. Engaging with diverse perspectives fosters empathy, understanding, and tolerance, broadening your worldview and enriching your social interactions.

Conclusion:

Building a supportive social network is a powerful investment in your well-being and resilience, providing a foundation of strength, connection, and belonging that sustains you through life's challenges. By nurturing meaningful relationships, fostering authenticity and reciprocity, and embracing diversity within your social circle, you can create a robust support system that enriches your life and helps you thrive in the face of adversity.

Overcoming Barriers to Relaxation

Clearing the Path to Inner Peace

In the pursuit of relaxation and tranquility, individuals often encounter various barriers that hinder their ability to unwind, recharge, and find solace amidst life's demands. These barriers, ranging from internal obstacles to external challenges, can impede the journey towards inner peace and well-being. By identifying and addressing common obstacles, individuals can pave the way for a sustainable relaxation plan that nurtures their mind, body, and soul.

Identifying and Addressing Common Obstacles:

Time Constraints: One of the most common barriers to relaxation is the perceived lack of time. Individuals may feel overwhelmed by their busy schedules, leaving little room for self-care and relaxation. To overcome this obstacle, it's essential to prioritize relaxation and carve out dedicated time for activities that promote well-being. This may involve scheduling relaxation sessions into your daily or weekly routine and setting boundaries to protect this time from other obligations.

Stressful Environments: External factors such as noisy surroundings, cluttered spaces, or chaotic environments can disrupt relaxation efforts. Creating a calming environment conducive to relaxation is key to overcoming this obstacle. Consider decluttering your living space, incorporating elements of nature such as plants or natural light, and minimizing distractions to create a peaceful sanctuary where you can unwind and rejuvenate.

Mindset and Beliefs: Negative thought patterns, self-limiting beliefs, and perfectionistic tendencies can sabotage relaxation efforts. Cultivating a positive mindset and challenging self-defeating thoughts is essential for overcoming this barrier. Practice self-compassion, cultivate gratitude, and embrace imperfection as part of the human experience. By adopting a growth-oriented mindset, individuals can create space for relaxation and self-care without feeling guilty or unworthy.

Physical Discomfort: Physical discomfort, such as tension, pain, or discomfort, can detract from relaxation efforts and contribute to feelings of agitation or restlessness. Addressing physical discomfort through techniques such as stretching, massage, or progressive muscle relaxation can help alleviate tension and promote relaxation. Additionally, practicing mindfulness and body awareness can help individuals tune into their bodies' signals and address discomfort before it escalates.

Creating a Sustainable Relaxation Plan:

Set Clear Goals and Intentions: Begin by clarifying your goals and intentions for relaxation. What do you hope to achieve through relaxation? Whether it's reducing stress, improving sleep, or enhancing overall well-being, setting clear intentions can guide your relaxation practices and keep you focused on your desired outcomes.

Incorporate Diverse Relaxation Techniques: Explore a variety of relaxation techniques to find what works best for you. This may include mindfulness meditation, deep breathing exercises, progressive muscle relaxation, yoga, tai chi, or guided imagery. Experiment with different practices to discover which ones resonate most with you and incorporate them into your relaxation plan.

Establish Consistent Routines: Consistency is key to reaping the benefits of relaxation. Establish consistent routines and rituals that signal to your body and mind that it's time to unwind. Whether it's a nightly relaxation ritual before bed or a weekly self-care routine, having predictable routines can help anchor your relaxation practices and make them a regular part of your life.

Practice Self-Compassion and Flexibility: Be gentle with yourself as you navigate the ups and downs of relaxation. Practice self-compassion and embrace flexibility in your approach, knowing that relaxation is not always linear and that it's okay to adjust your practices as needed. Allow yourself grace and kindness as you explore what works best for you on your journey towards inner peace and well-being.

Conclusion:

Overcoming barriers to relaxation requires a combination of self-awareness, intentionality, and perseverance. By identifying and addressing common obstacles, individuals can create a sustainable relaxation plan that nourishes their mind, body, and soul. With clarity of goals, diverse relaxation techniques, consistent routines, and a mindset of self-compassion and flexibility, individuals can clear the path to inner peace and cultivate a profound sense of well-being that enriches every aspect of their lives.

Mindful Parenting and Family Relaxation

Nurturing Harmony and Connection

In the whirlwind of modern family life, finding moments of relaxation and connection can feel like a distant dream. Yet, amidst the chaos, mindful parenting offers a path to cultivate harmony and tranquility within the family unit. By integrating mindfulness practices into everyday routines and prioritizing moments of shared relaxation, parents can foster a nurturing environment that promotes well-being for both themselves and their children.

Mindful Parenting:

Mindful parenting is rooted in the practice of present-moment awareness and non-judgmental acceptance. It involves being fully present and engaged with your children, tuning into their needs and emotions with compassion and understanding. By cultivating mindfulness in parenting, parents can respond to their children with greater patience, empathy, and authenticity, fostering deeper connections and promoting emotional resilience.

Family Relaxation Practices:

Integrating relaxation practices into family life offers an opportunity for parents and children to unwind together, bond, and create lasting memories. Whether it's through calming activities before bedtime, outdoor adventures in nature, or shared moments of mindfulness, family relaxation practices nourish the body, mind, and soul of each family member.

Creating a Relaxing Environment:

Setting the stage for family relaxation begins with creating a calming environment within the home. Designate spaces where family members can retreat to unwind and recharge, free from distractions and external pressures. Consider incorporating elements such as soft lighting, comfortable seating, soothing colors, and nature-inspired decor to create a peaceful atmosphere conducive to relaxation.

Mindful Activities for Families:

Nature Walks and Outdoor Adventures: Spend time exploring the great outdoors as a family, whether it's hiking through scenic trails, picnicking in local parks, or stargazing under the night sky. Nature offers a natural backdrop for mindfulness, inviting families to slow down, appreciate the beauty of the natural world, and connect with each other on a deeper level.

Mindful Eating: Transform mealtime into a mindful experience by savoring each bite and engaging all five senses. Encourage children to explore different flavors, textures, and aromas, fostering a sense of gratitude and appreciation for nourishing food. Create opportunities for family meals where everyone can come together, share stories, and enjoy each other's company without distractions.

Breathing Exercises and Guided Meditation: Practice simple breathing exercises and guided meditation sessions as a family to promote relaxation and stress relief. Set aside dedicated time each day for mindful breathing, inviting family members to focus on their breath and release tension from their bodies. Explore guided meditation apps or online resources designed specifically for children and families to make the practice accessible and engaging for all ages.

Creative Expression: Encourage creative expression as a means of relaxation and self-discovery. Provide art supplies, musical instruments, or writing materials for family members to explore their creative interests and express themselves freely. Engage in collaborative art projects, family jam sessions, or storytelling sessions to spark imagination and foster connection through shared creativity.

Conclusion:

Mindful parenting and family relaxation go hand in hand, offering a pathway to cultivate harmony, connection, and well-being within the family unit. By embracing mindfulness practices and incorporating moments of relaxation into everyday life, parents can create a nurturing environment where their children feel supported, cherished, and empowered to thrive. Together, families can embark on a journey of shared relaxation, bonding, and growth, creating cherished memories that will last a lifetime.

Introducing Relaxation Techniques to Children: Planting Seeds of Calm and Resilience

Teaching children relaxation techniques is a gift that empowers them with lifelong skills to navigate stress, manage emotions, and cultivate inner peace. By introducing simple yet effective relaxation practices at a young age, parents and caregivers can equip children with invaluable tools to thrive amidst life's challenges and promote overall well-being. Here's how to introduce relaxation techniques to children in a fun and engaging way:

1. Start with Breath Awareness:

Begin by teaching children the importance of breath awareness and its calming effects on the mind and body. Encourage them to take slow, deep breaths and notice how it makes them feel. Use playful imagery, such as blowing bubbles or pretending to blow out candles, to make breath awareness fun and engaging.

2. Practice Mindful Movement:

Incorporate mindful movement activities into daily routines, such as yoga, tai chi, or stretching exercises. Invite children to join in and explore different poses and movements while emphasizing the importance of being present in the moment and listening to their bodies.

3. Explore Guided Imagery:

Guide children through imaginative journeys using guided imagery techniques. Paint vivid pictures with words, describing peaceful scenes in nature or magical adventures in far-off lands. Encourage children to use their imagination to create their own mental landscapes where they feel safe, calm, and relaxed.

4. Foster Creativity with Art and Music:

Provide opportunities for creative expression through art and music activities. Offer coloring sheets, drawing materials, or musical instruments for children to explore their creativity and express their emotions in a nonverbal way. Encourage them to create art or music that reflects their feelings and helps them relax.

5. Establish Relaxation Rituals:

Create relaxation rituals that children can incorporate into their daily routines. Whether it's a bedtime meditation, a calming bath, or a soothing bedtime story, establish consistent practices that signal to children that it's time to unwind and relax. Make these rituals enjoyable and predictable to help children feel safe and secure.

6. Lead by Example:

Model relaxation techniques for children by practicing them yourself. Let children see you engage in mindfulness practices, such as deep breathing, meditation, or gentle movement exercises. Your own commitment to relaxation will inspire and encourage them to follow suit.

7. Make it Fun and Playful:

Infuse relaxation techniques with elements of play and imagination to keep children engaged and motivated. Use storytelling, games, or interactive activities to teach relaxation skills in a way that feels natural and enjoyable for children. Celebrate their efforts and progress along the way to reinforce positive associations with relaxation.

8. Encourage Regular Practice:

Encourage children to practice relaxation techniques regularly, incorporating them into their daily routine as a natural part of self-care. Celebrate their achievements and offer praise and encouragement to reinforce the importance of relaxation in promoting overall well-being.

Conclusion:

Introducing relaxation techniques to children is a journey of discovery, growth, and empowerment. By fostering a nurturing environment where relaxation is valued and practiced, parents and caregivers can help children develop essential skills to manage stress, regulate emotions, and thrive in all aspects of their lives. With patience, creativity, and a spirit of playfulness, children can cultivate a lifelong practice of relaxation that serves as a cornerstone of their well-being and resilience.

Fostering a Relaxing Family Environment: Cultivating Harmony and Connection

In the hustle and bustle of everyday life, creating a relaxing family environment is essential for promoting peace, harmony, and well-being. By intentionally designing spaces and routines that prioritize relaxation and connection, families can cultivate a sanctuary where they can unwind, recharge, and bond with one another. Here are some strategies for fostering a relaxing family environment:

1. Establish Tranquil Spaces:

Designate areas within your home that are dedicated to relaxation and tranquility. Create cozy nooks with comfortable seating, soft lighting, and soothing decor where family members can retreat to unwind and recharge. Consider incorporating elements of nature, such as indoor plants or natural materials, to evoke a sense of serenity and connection with the outdoors.

2. Minimize Clutter and Distractions:

Streamline your living spaces by minimizing clutter and eliminating unnecessary distractions. Create a calming environment free from visual and auditory clutter, such as excessive toys, electronic devices, or loud noises. Encourage family members to unplug from screens and engage in activities that promote relaxation and connection.

3. Establish Relaxation Rituals:

Establish daily or weekly relaxation rituals that bring the family together and promote a sense of calm and connection. This could include family meditation sessions, cozy movie nights, or bedtime storytelling sessions. Make these rituals a priority and set aside dedicated time to unwind and bond as a family.

4. Practice Mindful Communication:

Foster open, honest communication within your family by practicing mindful listening and empathy. Create a safe space where family members feel heard, valued, and respected. Encourage each other to express emotions and thoughts openly without judgment, and offer support and validation when needed.

5. Share Meals Together:

Make mealtimes a special occasion for family bonding by sharing meals together regularly. Turn off electronic devices, set the table with care, and enjoy each other's company over nourishing food. Use this time to catch up on each other's lives, share stories, and connect on a deeper level.

6. Embrace Nature and Outdoor Activities:

Spend time outdoors as a family, exploring nature and engaging in outdoor activities together. Whether it's going for a hike, having a picnic in the park, or simply playing in the backyard, immersing yourselves in nature can have a calming and rejuvenating effect on the entire family.

7. Encourage Relaxation Techniques:

Teach relaxation techniques to family members of all ages, such as deep breathing exercises, progressive muscle relaxation, or guided imagery. Practice these techniques together as a family to promote relaxation and stress relief. Encourage children to express their emotions and feelings in healthy ways, and provide support and guidance as needed.

8. Prioritize Self-Care:

Model self-care practices for your family by prioritizing your own well-being and setting boundaries around work and responsibilities. Encourage family members to engage in activities that promote self-care and relaxation, whether it's reading a book, taking a bubble bath, or going for a walk in nature.

Conclusion:

Creating a relaxing family environment requires intentionality, mindfulness, and a commitment to prioritizing well-being and connection. By implementing these strategies, families can create a sanctuary where they can unwind, recharge, and bond with one another amidst the busyness of everyday life. Together, families can cultivate a sense of peace, harmony, and togetherness that nourishes the body, mind, and soul.

The Workplace and Stress Reduction

Fostering a Culture of Well-being

In today's fast-paced and demanding work environments, stress has become a prevalent issue affecting employee well-being and organizational productivity. However, by prioritizing stress reduction initiatives and fostering a culture of well-being, workplaces can create environments where employees feel supported, engaged, and empowered to thrive. Here's how organizations can promote stress reduction in the workplace:

1. Cultivate a Supportive Work Culture:

Foster a work culture that values employee well-being and prioritizes mental health. Encourage open communication, empathy, and support among colleagues and leadership. Create an environment where employees feel comfortable discussing their stressors and seeking help when needed.

2. Provide Resources and Support:

Offer resources and support programs to help employees manage stress effectively. This could include access to counseling services, mindfulness training, stress management workshops, or employee assistance programs. Ensure that these resources are easily accessible and well-publicized within the organization.

3. Promote Work-Life Balance:

Encourage work-life balance by implementing flexible work arrangements, such as telecommuting, flexible hours, or compressed workweeks. Encourage employees to take regular breaks, use their vacation time, and disconnect from work outside of office hours. Lead by example by respecting boundaries and promoting a healthy work-life balance among leadership.

4. Foster a Positive Work Environment:

Create a positive and supportive work environment that promotes collaboration, recognition, and appreciation. Celebrate achievements, acknowledge employee contributions, and foster a sense of belonging within the organization. Encourage teamwork, camaraderie, and mutual respect among colleagues.

5. Provide Opportunities for Skill Development:

Offer opportunities for skill development and career growth to empower employees and enhance their sense of control and competence. Invest in training programs, professional development opportunities, and leadership coaching to help employees build resilience and adaptability in the face of workplace challenges.

6. Encourage Physical Activity and Wellness:

Promote physical activity and wellness initiatives to help employees manage stress and improve their overall health and well-being. Offer onsite fitness classes, wellness challenges, or subsidies for gym memberships. Create a culture that values and prioritizes employee health and encourages regular exercise and movement breaks throughout the workday.

7. Foster a Sense of Purpose and Meaning:

Help employees connect to the broader purpose and mission of the organization, fostering a sense of meaning and fulfillment in their work. Communicate organizational goals and values clearly, and provide opportunities for employees to contribute to meaningful projects and initiatives. Encourage employees to align their work with their personal values and passions.

8. Prioritize Managerial Support and Leadership:

Train managers and leaders to recognize signs of stress and support employees in managing their workload and responsibilities effectively. Encourage managers to lead by example, prioritize employee well-being, and foster a culture of trust, respect, and psychological safety within their teams.

Conclusion:

By prioritizing stress reduction initiatives and fostering a culture of well-being, workplaces can create environments where employees feel valued, supported, and empowered to thrive. By cultivating a supportive work culture, providing resources and support, promoting work-life balance, fostering a positive work environment, offering opportunities for skill development, encouraging physical activity and wellness, fostering a sense of purpose and meaning, and prioritizing managerial support and leadership, organizations can promote stress reduction and enhance employee well-being and organizational success.

Implementing Relaxation Strategies in the Workplace and Creating a Stress-Resilient Work Environment

In today's fast-paced work environments, stress has become a common concern that can negatively impact employee well-being and organizational productivity. However, by implementing relaxation strategies and creating a stress-resilient work environment, employers can support their employees in managing stress effectively and fostering a culture of well-being. Here's how organizations can implement relaxation strategies and create a stress-resilient work environment:

1. Establish Relaxation Zones:

Designate specific areas within the workplace as relaxation zones where employees can unwind and recharge during breaks. Equip these areas with comfortable seating, soothing decor, and amenities such as noise-canceling headphones or calming music to create a peaceful atmosphere conducive to relaxation.

2. Offer Mindfulness Training:

Provide mindfulness training programs or workshops to help employees develop mindfulness skills and techniques for managing stress. Teach employees how to practice mindfulness meditation, deep breathing exercises, and other relaxation techniques that promote present-moment awareness and stress reduction.

3. Encourage Regular Breaks:

Encourage employees to take regular breaks throughout the workday to rest and recharge. Encourage them to step away from their desks, go for a short walk, or engage in brief relaxation exercises to reduce stress and improve focus and productivity.

4. Implement Flexible Work Arrangements:

Offer flexible work arrangements such as remote work options, flexible hours, or compressed workweeks to help employees better manage their work-life balance. Providing flexibility in how and where work is done can help reduce stress and improve overall well-being.

5. Foster Social Connections:

Create opportunities for social connections and camaraderie among employees by organizing team-building activities, social events, or group outings. Building strong relationships and a sense of belonging within the workplace can help buffer against stress and promote resilience.

6. Provide Stress Management Resources:

Offer resources and support services to help employees manage stress effectively. This could include access to counseling services, employee assistance programs, or online resources and tools for stress management and resilience building.

7. Lead by Example:

Leadership plays a crucial role in creating a stress-resilient work environment. Lead by example by prioritizing self-care, taking regular breaks, and modeling healthy work habits. Encourage open communication and provide support to employees experiencing stress or burnout.

8. Promote Work-Life Integration:

Encourage employees to integrate work and personal life in a way that promotes balance and well-being. Provide support for managing caregiving responsibilities, pursuing hobbies and interests outside of work, and prioritizing self-care activities that promote relaxation and stress reduction.

9. Conduct Stress Assessments:

Regularly assess workplace stress levels through employee surveys, focus groups, or one-on-one discussions to identify areas of concern and opportunities for improvement. Use this feedback to tailor relaxation strategies and interventions to meet the specific needs of employees.

10. Celebrate Successes and Milestones:

Recognize and celebrate successes and milestones achieved by individuals and teams within the organization. Express gratitude and appreciation for employees' hard work and contributions, fostering a positive and supportive work environment that promotes resilience and well-being.

Conclusion:

By implementing relaxation strategies and creating a stress-resilient work environment, organizations can support their employees in managing stress effectively and promoting overall well-being. By establishing relaxation zones, offering mindfulness training, encouraging regular breaks, implementing flexible work arrangements, fostering social connections, providing stress management resources, leading by example, promoting work-life integration, conducting stress assessments, and celebrating successes and milestones, employers can create a workplace culture that prioritizes employee well-being and resilience.

Maintaining Relaxation Practices Over Time

Sustaining Well-being in a Busy World

Incorporating relaxation practices into our daily routines is a powerful tool for managing stress, enhancing overall well-being, and promoting resilience. However, maintaining these practices over time can be challenging, especially in the face of busy schedules and competing demands. Here are some strategies for sustaining relaxation practices over time:

1. Establish Consistent Routines:

Create consistent routines that incorporate relaxation practices into your daily schedule. Set aside dedicated time each day for relaxation, whether it's in the morning before work, during lunch breaks, or in the evening before bed. Consistency is key to forming lasting habits.

2. Start Small and Build Gradually:

Begin with manageable relaxation practices that fit into your lifestyle and gradually build upon them over time. Start with just a few minutes of deep breathing or mindfulness meditation each day and gradually increase the duration or complexity of your practices as you become more comfortable.

3. Be Flexible and Adaptive:

Be flexible and adaptive in your approach to relaxation practices, recognizing that life can be unpredictable and schedules may change. Find creative ways to incorporate relaxation into different settings and situations, whether it's during your commute, while waiting in line, or during short breaks throughout the day.

4. Find What Works for You:

Explore different relaxation techniques and find what works best for you. Whether it's yoga, meditation, progressive muscle relaxation, or guided imagery, choose practices that resonate with you personally and bring you a sense of calm and relaxation.

5. Prioritize Self-Care:

Prioritize self-care as an essential aspect of maintaining relaxation practices over time. Recognize the importance of taking care of yourself physically, mentally, and emotionally, and make self-care a non-negotiable part of your daily routine.

6. Seek Accountability and Support:

Find accountability partners or support groups who share similar goals and can provide encouragement and motivation along the way. Whether it's joining a meditation group, attending yoga classes with friends, or participating in online communities, surround yourself with a supportive network that can help keep you accountable.

7. Practice Mindfulness in Everyday Life:

Incorporate mindfulness into your everyday activities by bringing awareness to the present moment and infusing moments of daily life with mindfulness practices. Whether it's eating mindfully, practicing mindful walking, or engaging in everyday tasks with full awareness, find opportunities to cultivate mindfulness throughout your day.

8. Reflect on Your Progress:

Take time to reflect on your progress and celebrate your successes along the way. Acknowledge the benefits of relaxation practices in your life, whether it's reduced stress, improved sleep, enhanced focus, or greater overall well-being. Use these reflections as motivation to continue your journey.

9. Be Kind to Yourself:

Be kind to yourself and practice self-compassion as you navigate the ups and downs of maintaining relaxation practices over time. Recognize that setbacks are a natural part of the process and that it's okay to occasionally veer off course. Approach yourself with gentleness and understanding, and commit to returning to your practices with renewed dedication.

10. Stay Connected to Your Why:

Stay connected to your why – the reasons why you embarked on this journey of self-care and relaxation in the first place. Whether it's to reduce stress, improve health, or cultivate greater peace and joy in your life, remind yourself of your motivations regularly to stay focused and committed to your practices.

Conclusion:

Maintaining relaxation practices over time requires commitment, dedication, and a willingness to adapt to life's changes and challenges. By establishing consistent routines, starting small and building gradually, being flexible and adaptive, finding what works for you, prioritizing self-care, seeking accountability and support, practicing mindfulness in everyday life, reflecting on your progress, being kind to yourself, and staying connected to your why, you can sustain relaxation practices and cultivate a greater sense of well-being and resilience in the long term.

Strategies for Long-Term Relaxation Success: Cultivating Sustainable Well-being

Long-term relaxation success involves implementing strategies that not only initiate relaxation practices but also sustain them over time, ensuring lasting benefits for overall well-being. Here are key strategies for achieving long-term relaxation success:

1. Establish Clear Goals:

Define clear and achievable goals for your relaxation journey. Determine what specific outcomes you hope to achieve, whether it's reducing stress, improving sleep, enhancing mood, or fostering greater overall well-being. Having clear goals provides direction and motivation for your relaxation practices.

2. Develop Consistent Habits:

Cultivate consistent habits by integrating relaxation practices into your daily routine. Set aside dedicated time each day for relaxation, whether it's in the morning, during breaks throughout the day, or in the evening before bed. Consistency is essential for building lasting habits that contribute to long-term relaxation success.

3. Start Small and Progress Gradually:

Begin with small, manageable steps and gradually progress as you become more comfortable with your relaxation practices. Start with simple techniques such as deep breathing or mindfulness meditation and gradually increase the duration or complexity of your practices over time. Incremental progress ensures sustainable integration into your lifestyle.

4. Practice Self-Compassion:

Be gentle and compassionate with yourself as you navigate your relaxation journey. Accept that setbacks and challenges are a natural part of the process, and approach yourself with kindness and understanding. Practice self-compassion during times of difficulty, acknowledging your efforts and resilience along the way.

5. Stay Flexible and Adaptive:

Remain flexible and adaptable in your approach to relaxation practices, recognizing that life is dynamic and ever-changing. Be willing to adjust your routines and practices to accommodate shifting schedules, priorities, and circumstances. Embrace a mindset of adaptability to sustain your relaxation journey over the long term.

6. Cultivate Mindfulness in Daily Life:

Integrate mindfulness into your everyday activities by bringing awareness to the present moment. Practice mindfulness during routine tasks such as eating, walking, or commuting, infusing moments of daily life with mindfulness practices. Cultivating mindfulness in daily life enhances your overall well-being and supports long-term relaxation success.

7. Seek Accountability and Support:

Surround yourself with a supportive network of friends, family, or peers who can offer encouragement and accountability on your relaxation journey. Share your goals and progress with others, and enlist their support in staying committed to your practices.

Accountability and support from others can bolster your motivation and resilience.

8. Reflect on Progress and Celebrate Milestones:

Take time to reflect on your progress and celebrate milestones along the way. Acknowledge the positive changes and benefits that result from your relaxation practices, whether it's reduced stress, improved mood, or greater resilience. Celebrating your achievements reinforces your commitment to long-term relaxation success.

9. Prioritize Self-Care:

Make self-care a priority in your life by nurturing your physical, mental, and emotional well-being. Attend to your needs through activities that replenish and rejuvenate you, whether it's exercise, hobbies, social connections, or relaxation practices. Prioritizing self-care ensures that you maintain a strong foundation for long-term relaxation success.

10. Stay Connected to Your Purpose:

Stay connected to your underlying purpose and motivations for engaging in relaxation practices. Remind yourself of the reasons why relaxation is important to you and the positive impact it has on your life. Staying connected to your purpose fuels your commitment and resilience, sustaining you on your journey toward long-term relaxation success.

Conclusion:

Achieving long-term relaxation success requires commitment, consistency, and a supportive mindset. By establishing clear goals, developing consistent habits, starting small and progressing gradually, practicing self-compassion, staying flexible and adaptive, cultivating mindfulness in daily life, seeking accountability and support, reflecting on progress and celebrating milestones, prioritizing self-care, and staying connected to your purpose, you can cultivate sustainable well-being and resilience through relaxation practices that endure over time.

Integrating Relaxation into Daily Life

Integrating relaxation into daily life involves incorporating techniques and practices that promote calmness, mindfulness, and stress reduction into your everyday routines. Here are several approaches you can take to integrate relaxation into your daily life:

1. Morning Rituals:

Start your day with calming morning rituals that set a positive tone for the rest of the day. This could include practices such as meditation, deep breathing exercises, gentle stretching, or journaling. Take a few moments to center yourself and cultivate a sense of peace before diving into your daily activities.

2. Mindful Moments:

Throughout the day, create mindful moments to pause, breathe, and bring awareness to the present moment. Whether you're waiting in line, commuting to work, or taking a break between tasks, use these moments as opportunities to practice mindfulness. Take a few deep breaths, observe your surroundings, and tune into your senses to anchor yourself in the present moment.

3. Incorporate Movement:

Integrate movement into your daily routine as a form of relaxation and stress relief. This could involve activities such as walking, yoga, tai chi, or dancing. Find opportunities to move your body mindfully, whether it's taking a walk during your lunch break, practicing yoga in the morning, or dancing to your favorite music in the evening.

4. Create Breathing Breaks:

Take regular breathing breaks throughout the day to reset and recharge your mind and body. Practice deep breathing exercises to activate the body's relaxation response and calm the nervous system. Set reminders on your phone or computer to prompt you to take breathing breaks at regular intervals.

5. Mindful Eating:

Practice mindful eating as a way to cultivate relaxation and savor your food more fully. Slow down and pay attention to each bite, noticing the flavors, textures, and sensations of the food. Chew slowly, and try to eat without distractions, allowing yourself to fully engage with the experience of eating.

6. Unplug and Disconnect:

Dedicate time each day to unplug from technology and disconnect from digital distractions. Create tech-free zones or periods of time where you intentionally step away from screens and devices. Use this time to engage in activities that promote relaxation and connection, such as reading, spending time outdoors, or enjoying hobbies.

7. Practice Gratitude:

Cultivate a practice of gratitude as a way to shift your focus from stress to appreciation. Take a few moments each day to reflect on the things you're grateful for, whether it's small moments of joy, supportive relationships, or simple pleasures. Practicing gratitude can help foster a positive mindset and reduce stress levels.

8. Wind Down in the Evening:

Establish calming bedtime rituals to help you unwind and prepare for a restful night's sleep. This could include activities such as gentle stretching, reading a book, taking a warm bath, or practicing relaxation techniques such as progressive muscle relaxation or guided imagery. Create a soothing bedtime routine that signals to your body and mind that it's time to relax and prepare for sleep.

9. Set Boundaries and Prioritize Self-Care:

Set boundaries around your time and energy to prioritize self-care and relaxation. Learn to say no to activities or commitments that drain you and prioritize activities that nourish and replenish you. Make self-care a non-negotiable part of your daily routine, and honor your need for rest and relaxation.

10. Reflect and Adjust:

Take time to reflect on your daily routines and habits, and make adjustments as needed to better support your well-being. Notice what activities or practices bring you the most relaxation and incorporate more of them into your daily life. Be open to experimentation and exploration as you find what works best for you.

By integrating relaxation into your daily life in these ways, you can cultivate a greater sense of calm, mindfulness, and well-being amidst the busyness of modern life.

Conclusion: Embracing The Art of Relaxation

In the journey of life, amidst the hustle and bustle of daily demands, embracing the art of relaxation becomes not just a luxury but a necessity for our overall well-being. As we've explored various techniques, strategies, and approaches to relaxation, it becomes clear that relaxation is not merely about taking breaks or escaping from our responsibilities, but rather about cultivating a deeper sense of presence, balance, and harmony in our lives.

Through practices such as mindfulness meditation, deep breathing exercises, yoga, creative expression, and connecting with nature, we can tap into the innate capacity within us to unwind, recharge, and replenish our energy reserves. Relaxation is not a one-size-fits-all solution but rather a personalized journey that invites us to explore what resonates with our unique preferences, needs, and lifestyles.

By integrating relaxation into our daily routines and prioritizing self-care, we can navigate the ups and downs of life with greater resilience, grace, and ease. We learn to listen to the whispers of our bodies and minds, honoring our need for rest, rejuvenation, and renewal amidst the constant motion of the world around us.

As we conclude our exploration of the art of relaxation, let us remember that relaxation is not just a destination to reach but a continual practice to cultivate. It is a lifelong journey of self-discovery, self-care, and self-compassion, inviting us to embrace the present moment with openness, curiosity, and kindness.

May we carry the wisdom of relaxation into all aspects of our lives, fostering greater well-being, connection, and joy in each moment. And may we continue to nurture the art of relaxation not only for ourselves but also for the benefit of those around us, creating ripple effects of peace and serenity in our communities and beyond.

In embracing the art of relaxation, we embrace the fullness of life itself – embracing the beauty of stillness amidst the chaos, the serenity of silence amidst the noise, and the profound sense of peace that arises when we simply allow ourselves to be.

Let us journey forward with open hearts and relaxed minds, knowing that within the depths of our being lies an oasis of calmness and tranquility, waiting to be discovered and embraced.

Here's to the art of relaxation – may it guide us, nourish us, and inspire us to live each moment with presence, purpose, and profound peace.

Reflecting on the Journey and Moving Forward with a Relaxation Mindset

As we pause to reflect on our journey of exploring relaxation techniques and strategies, it's essential to acknowledge the progress we've made and the insights we've gained along the way. Each step taken, each breath consciously drawn, has contributed to our growth and well-being, paving the path toward a more relaxed and balanced life.

In looking back, we may recognize moments of transformation, where stress gave way to serenity, and tension dissolved into tranquility. We've discovered the power of mindfulness, the healing potential of self-care, and the profound impact of nurturing our mind-body connection. Through this journey, we've learned that relaxation is not merely a destination but a way of being – a mindset that infuses every aspect of our lives with calmness, clarity, and compassion.

As we move forward, let us carry with us the lessons learned and the practices cultivated, embracing a relaxation mindset that permeates our thoughts, actions, and interactions. Let us remember that relaxation is not an end goal but an ongoing practice – a daily commitment to ourselves and our well-being.

With this relaxation mindset, we approach life's challenges with greater resilience and grace, knowing that we have the tools to navigate stress and uncertainty with calmness and confidence. We prioritize self-care as a non-negotiable aspect of our daily routine, honoring our need for rest, rejuvenation, and renewal.

Moving forward with a relaxation mindset also means cultivating awareness and presence in each moment, savoring the simple joys of life and finding moments of peace amidst the busyness of daily life. It means letting go of perfectionism and embracing imperfection, recognizing that true relaxation comes from acceptance and surrender.

As we embark on the next phase of our journey, let us continue to explore and experiment with relaxation techniques, remaining open to new possibilities and experiences. Let us seek inspiration from nature, art, music, and other sources of beauty and tranquility that nourish our soul.

And let us remember that we are not alone on this journey – we have a supportive community of fellow travelers, friends, and loved ones who share in our commitment to relaxation and well-being. Together, we can uplift and empower each other, creating a ripple effect of peace and serenity in our lives and the world around us.

In conclusion, reflecting on our journey and moving forward with a relaxation mindset reminds us that relaxation is not a destination to reach but a way of life to embrace. It is a journey of self-discovery, growth, and transformation – a journey that leads us back to ourselves, to the essence of who we are beneath the layers of stress and distraction.

May we continue to walk this path with courage, curiosity, and compassion, knowing that each step taken brings us closer to a life of greater ease, balance, and well-being. And may the relaxation mindset guide us, support us, and inspire us to live each moment with presence, purpose, and profound peace.

Author

Harmony Grace is actively involved in promoting well-being through workshops, online resources, and a supportive community. Her commitment to fostering a sense of harmony extends beyond the pages of the book, creating an ongoing dialogue with readers seeking to embark on their own journey toward relaxation and self-discovery.

The author brings a wealth of knowledge and a soothing presence to the exploration of relaxation and self-care. Drawing from a background in psychology, wellness coaching, and personal development, she is deeply committed to helping individuals navigate the complexities of modern life with grace and calm.

Milton Keynes UK
Ingram Content Group UK Ltd.
UKHW011157110324
439162UK00015B/100